ISBN: 1500701653
ISBN-13: 978-1500701659

SYNOPSIS

PART ONE

Introduction

Chapter One. Early Experiences

Chapter Two. Early Healing and Other Experiences

Chapter Three. Dangerous Encounters

Chapter Four. Controlling Healing Powers

Chapter Five. The Loneliness of the Healer

Chapter Six. The Word Spreads

Chapter Seven. Challenges ... and Perks

Chapter Eight. Spirits in Limbo

Chapter Nine. Mediation

Chapter Ten. The Light

Chapter Eleven. Learning to Shut Down

PART TWO

Chapter Twelve. "Patients'" Stories

Chapter Thirteen. "Patients" at Work

Acknowledgements

SYNOPSIS

THE EIGHTH SENSE?

'The Eighth Sense?' is the story of an ordinary man who has two extraordinary gifts.

The first gift is of healing. He tells of the many people he has helped in lots of different ways and in a variety of places - even the middle of a road on one occasion. Although, understandably, he doesn't remember each individual case, he reckons the number must be in the region of a thousand. Several of these people have written their own accounts of what happened and these are included in this book.

He doesn't claim to cure everyone's pain or that his healing always has a permanent effect but his special gifts have improved the lives of many who have received his warming touch. Nor does he claim that it is he who is the healer - he always asks the recipient to say 'thank you' to whoever or whatever they believe in and emphasises that he is just the channel for the power that heals.

The second, sometimes unwelcome, gift is that he is a psychic. This side of his story relates some of his numerous encounters with spirits or ghosts and is sometimes funny, sometimes sad, sometimes scary - but always fascinating. He has encountered Tudor ghosts in Hampton Court, a young boy who drowned in a swimming pool and a suicide who tried to kill him. He had his first encounter with a spirit - a prolonged one - at seven years of age.

Each gift imposes a heavy burden and Pinky has had to learn how to cope with it and shield himself from potential harmful effects, such as hostility and incredulity from family and friends, plus physical pain and mental anguish.

Pinky's matter of fact approach to his more unusual encounters as a result of both of his gifts lends a charm to his story and a touch of enigma. He talks of driving with a ghost sitting beside him in the passenger seat as if this were an everyday occurrence. He does, however, think it a bit of a liberty when spirits take over his body and use him as a mouthpiece when they want to talk to someone still living.

Pinky acquired his life-long nick-name from his father, who called his three sons Inky, Pinky and Ponky after the 1940s rhyme, *Inky, Pinky, Ponky/ Daddy bought a donkey/ The donkey died/ And Daddy cried/ Inky, Pinky, Ponky.*

PART ONE

INTRODUCTION

I knew from an early age that I was somehow different, though not exactly how or why. I was aware of seeing and feeling 'things' but, in my innocence, didn't fully realise that nobody else around me could.

I don't expect everybody to believe my story, "each to their own" as they say. It must be hard to accept that someone as normal as I am can communicate with people who are no longer here on earth - if it wasn't me, I probably wouldn't believe it either. The 'people' I see are usually in limbo. They don't realise they have passed and I am more than willing to help them go towards the light into which our spirits go when we die, to be with their loved ones once again.

There are different types of spirits. Some are there standing next to you. Some you see and some you don't. Those you don't see you don't think about unless they make their presence felt or appear to threaten you.

I can't choose who I see, it's random, otherwise I would chat with Marilyn Monroe or Elvis and ask them how <u>did</u> they die. No, it's not like that at all, maybe other psychics can, but I can't.

Neither do I claim to be able to heal everyone. I am not God. Some people who ask for help have what seems like a mental brick wall surrounding them which is impossible to get through. Maybe these people are subconsciously afraid of the unknown (it's understandable) but I don't know. What I do know is that I can heal some people and alleviate the aches and pains of others temporarily or sometimes permanently. I don't claim to cure people who are terminally ill, but I can ease the discomfort of their symptoms.

I appreciate the non-believers. My experiences have never been easy to get my head round and when it all began I struggled with belief myself until I realised that it was coming from a source outside me and then I was able to believe. Open your hearts and minds - you may just be surprised by what you find. This world really is full of wonders. Embrace all you can while you can.

Chapter One

Early Experiences

When I was a kid I shared a bedroom with my younger brother and every night I used to see a woman (a spirit) standing at the end of my bed. I never told my mum or my dad about that - I'm not sure why. I was about six or seven and often the woman used to sit on my brother's bed and I would stare at her most of the night and she would stare right back at me; that freaked me out. Back then, I didn't think to say anything to her. I just tried to pretend that she wasn't there, but I knew she was because my brother used to get scared (he could sense but not see her). He'd say "Get into bed with me because I'm scared" and I used to get into his bed and cuddle him until he went to sleep and then get back into my own bed. He still speaks about it and remembers me getting into bed and putting my arms round him till he went to sleep.

I used to put the light on so that the woman disappeared but my mum or dad would get up and say "Who's left the light on?" and turn it off; so then I'd be hiding under the sheets and peeping out to look at her watching me again.

It was really tough, I was always in trouble at school. When I went to school in the morning I used to fall asleep during class and there was a certain teacher who always used to whack me round the head and say "King, wake up".

Every night I would go to bed knowing that I would see this old woman with lots of long grey hair done up into a bun and wearing a sort of grey raincoat. She never appeared to be trying to talk to me; she just stared at me - bang in the eyes; it was a very unpleasant sort of stare. At the time we were living in a block of flats in Mortlake. I was about seven when this started and it went on for years. It is, I suppose, surprising that I didn't tell someone in the family or at school as I was afraid of getting into trouble. Perhaps this came from the nature of this 'gift' in that it took over and didn't connect with rational thought - or maybe I was afraid nobody would believe me and people would laugh at me.

Then, when I was eleven and just about to start secondary school, she just disappeared - one day she just wasn't there any more. This was a great relief to me and I hope that she found her way to the light and moved on.

My parents were astrologers. They had no religious beliefs. They were not church-going people. The only time I went to church was to sing in the choir at weddings. I used to get paid half a crown which was a lot of money then. Astrology left me cold, I never had time for it. As a kid I listened to be polite, I suppose, but never got interested in it. Yet perhaps something in their psyche passed into my genes to become this special ability.

*****

I left school. I did an apprenticeship as an electrician and got my City and Guilds. My older brother pushed me into that. When we were kids we used to fight all the time, largely because I used to nick his clothes, and he was always talking down to me. That's when I learned to fight - I learned to be tough. In those days everyone went around in gangs; I was a skinhead. I went out with a lot of girls and did a few things which I regret now and wonder why I did them.

Then I met Elaine …

When I was twenty-one, I met my future wife in the unemployment centre - I was just signing on, she was sixteen. I fell in love with her. We both got jobs; she worked in an office and I got a job as a labourer. Elaine and I moved in together to a little flat in Kew when she was nineteen and I was twenty-three. We are still together after thirty years.

Over some time my work with the builders changed and I eventually settled as a painter and decorator, a job which I am good at and enjoy doing. In a curious way my job seems to act as a vehicle for both my 'gifts' from time to time, perhaps because it takes me to a wide variety of places and introduces me to many different people.

Sometimes I become aware that the person in the place in which I'm working is in pain or has a problem that I know I can help them with and in that case I usually suggest they let me help. For some people the idea "freaks" them and they say "No", but as often as not they let me.

There are times when I sense a "presence" in the house; usually these are benign souls who have simply not found the way to move on but sometimes, thankfully rarely, they are bitter, twisted and full of hatred and malign power and on those occasions I'm afraid. Imagine being an adult and being terrified. Nobody should be terrified of anything but there are many terrifying things and I don't know why I should want to see them, but they are there and I do. I used to get up every day and wonder what was going to happen. At one point I thought I was going mad (my wife thought I was, too) but I found books on the subject and discovered that there were other people who had had similar experiences and they helped me realise that I'm not mad. Amongst the books that have helped me through the years are two by Jackie Newcomb (*An Angel Treasury* and *An Angel By My Side*) and two by Richard Webster (*Spirit Guides* and *Angel Guardians*). Several people I have met over the years have helped me to come to terms with it too and have shown me how to defend myself against a malign power. There are a surprising number of people who have similar experiences both of spirits (ghosts) and of healing.

My family don't wish to acknowledge the healing that I do, which I find difficult to cope with - although they do ask for help from time to time. They know about it but are unwilling to talk about it, probably because they are embarrassed; they don't like to hear me talk about it either. I suppose we all like to feel comfortable in our own community environment where to be noticed for being particularly good at something like sport or music is normal and acceptable, but not for something 'strange'. Some of the incidents with evil spirits have been very frightening indeed and I've felt the need to tell someone about it right away. This happened with the experience told in *Chapter Three*. It happened on a day when one of our boys was playing football as he did regularly. The parents used to meet every week and the fathers would go to the pub. On this particular day I was still shaking from the encounter I had had and made the mistake of telling the other fathers what had happened … when I had finished they started to slip away. They obviously thought I was mad and I can't really blame them. It just illustrates what an isolating experience all this can be - most people can't relate to something like that.

Chapter Two

Early Healing and Other Experiences

It is surprising how many houses have ghosts still lingering. In the first flat my wife and I lived in together I saw a woman who appeared to be levitating so that her head nearly touched the ceiling. I didn't tell Elaine about it because I was afraid she wouldn't move in with me. This was only relatively minor, so I didn't let it get to me too much. The woman was there all the time but I only saw her when I went to bed. I always kept the light on (even though the meter needed to be fed), and Elaine used to ask why I was scared, even though I'm a grown man.

When I first saw this woman in spirit form, I was unnerved. I never tried to speak to her or ask her why she was there. We were in the flat for five years and she was still there when we left. Neither of my kids saw the woman, they were too young. Even though I now know how to do it, I don't want to go back and send her away because I can sense that she is one of those spirits who wants to stay. There are many spirits out there who are quite happy to stay. On the other hand a lot of these souls are stuck and these are happy to be helped. But to go around sending everybody on their way would be a bit much!

*****

We moved because we now had two kids in a one-bedroom flat. When we moved I didn't think to check the new house first for spirit presences, but luckily there weren't any. The eleven years we spent there were very happy times. The house backed onto a cemetery and to go to work I was picked up on the other side of it. The cemetery was surrounded by a high wall. In order to get to the pick-up place on time I used to take a short-cut by jumping over the wall and running, taking a different route each day. This was a routine I got used to, and it went on for eleven years. People may well wonder why I was unaffected by living next to a cemetery … maybe it was because the spirits were peacefully at rest.

*****

My sister-in-law's dog, Holly, died and she got a German Shepherd (my favourite breed) a bitch called Scarlett. She wasn't scared of anything but when, in the evening, my sister-in-law and my mother-in-law would come round to my house the dog absolutely refused to go out into the back garden. My mother- and sister-in-law thought this was because of the cemetery and that the dog felt the ghosts but that reason had not registered with me. I did feel it, but I was fine with it, something told me it was OK, maybe because I was used to walking through the cemetery ... I don't know. I was not conscious that I was getting to know the spirits. I was content just reading the names, when they died and how old they were. Some of the stonework of the graves looked very good. I varied the route each day because I enjoyed looking at different graves, and it was a nice diversion from the everyday grind. I was not really aware of the spirits at that point. The psychic side of me had not fully surfaced.

Scarlett really liked me and would follow me around. Later I did some healing on the dog (she had gut problems and was getting mange) and ever since then she never leaves me alone when I am in the house with her - she will whine for ten minutes or so when I arrive and then sit near me watching me.

My sister-in-law writes about it:

> "I have a twelve year old German Shepherd named Scarlett. When she was about six years old she began to itch over her paws, legs and body - practically all over. She had sarcoptic mange.
>
> My brother-in-law, who is a healer, offered to see if he could cure her; I agreed that he should have a go. One evening he came over to my mum's house and placed his hand on Scarlett's body. After a few minutes she looked at him and then looked away. When my brother-in-law finished his healing, she went to her bed

and slept, as she seemed very tired. My brother-in-law repeated the healing over the course of a few days and the mange seemed to disappear.

The healing seemed to work for Scarlett, but I think it depends on the animal and if she/he trusts the healer. In my opinion it is worth a go BUT seek a vet's opinion as well. This is an extremely bad skin condition and the animal will suffer if you do not act quickly."

*****

I think that the easiest healing I have done has been on animals (I have healed two, the other one was our cat) they don't have any of the resistance to unusual things which people have. We see this in the simple trust they show and the ease with which they build bonds with us.

*****

We went on holiday to Turkey one year with the kids. We have three cats and my sister-in-law was feeding them for us while we were away and she noticed that one of the cats, Chelsea, had a huge lump on his cheek. Anyway when we got back we walked in through the door and Chelsea had a massive hole in his face beside the lump and you could actually see the bone poking through. I thought 'Oh no, not this, this will cost us £400 that we haven't got' … and it was late at night. I put my hand over his cheek and the cat didn't run off so I held my hand there for about five minutes.

I said "We'll wait till morning and we'll just have to take it to the vet no matter what because we can't leave the cat like this".

So the kids went to bed and we followed soon afterwards. We came down in the morning and the cat … not only was it healed, but its fur had grown back as well, there wasn't even a mark there! My wife said that for the first time she really believed in me because, out of everything I've ever done, that was the most amazing thing she had seen.

My wife tells the story:

> "I knew Pinky had a "gift", but didn't really take much interest. I found it slightly embarrassing to be honest and hated the attention it caused. I thought people would think he was a freak and I couldn't bear the thought that our kids would suffer. Nevertheless, I went along with it all to a certain

extent … but it caused plenty of arguments!

We went away to Turkey for a week and my sister fed our three cats. On our return she left a message saying that one of them (Chelsea) had a badly swollen cheek and on seeing him I knew he needed to see the vet the very next day. He looked as though he had an orange in his cheek. 'Great' I thought, 'that's all I need - a bloody vet's bill'! That night I remember Pinky placing his hand over Chelsea's head for about five minutes, but didn't think much of it.

Next morning I woke knowing I had to get the cat to the vet as soon as possible - I hated the thought that he could be in pain. I remember making the tea and Chelsea walking towards me … I glanced at his cheek and froze. The lump was completely gone! I felt dizzy and slightly sick. It was amazing, nothing short of a miracle! Despite Pinky helping so many people, this, to me, was living proof that he really did have a gift. I suppose I subconsciously thought that people sometimes believe what they want to believe and are prone to a little exaggeration, whereas animals can't.

Before my cynical eyes, I saw my husband heal our cat. Despite being a little freaked, I had, at last, to give Pink the benefit of the doubt - he could heal and, what's more, he saved us a small fortune in vet's fees!"

Since then, Chelsea sleeps with my daughter, but during the day he sleeps under the loft hatch - an awkward position because it is at the top of the stairs as you turn round. The cat is always there and I know he sleeps there because of the man in the loft (see below). He never did that before I healed him. There are four beds he could sleep on, but the cat chooses to lie there - it's not even a comfortable piece of carpet because there is no underlay under it! The man is not a bad entity but I have a funny feeling that the cat is protection for the house.

Although there is a spirit in this house (the man who stays in the loft) he doesn't bother me and I don't mind him being there. I was not aware of him when we first moved in. He's quite happy being there. The only time he troubles me is at Christmas when I go up to the loft to get the Christmas tree and then I prefer to take my youngest son with me to give me a hand.

Sometimes people are half aware of spirits around them but do not allow it to register in their everyday consciousness. My third son is aware of the spirit in the loft of the house we now live in but doesn't really take it on board and I avoid talking about it because I don't want him, or the other kids, to be scared. Now that he is older I think that if the subject comes up again I'll let him talk about it. The rest of my family are unwilling to accept the encounters I have had with spirits.

*****

One time one of my sons had done something quite bad to his knee playing football and he asked, really aggressively, whether I could 'do' his knee. I said I didn't think so and he said "Well why don't you try, you do other people so why can't you do me?"

Before, even when he'd been ill or hurt himself and I'd said to him "Come here a minute", he used to say "Get off me, don't you touch me with your stuff". That's what he's been like. I think he's embarrassed because friends and neighbours have said that his dad heals people.

However, his knee was really bad - he was nearly crying with the pain - and he said "All right, go on then. Go on, see what you can do with it". I placed my hand over his knee for five minutes and the swelling went down and the pain went away.

My son doesn't like talking about it at all now. I suppose it's hard for people who don't have this gift to accept it and, of course, young people in particular want to be seen as normal and they shy away from anything that is out of the ordinary.

All in all, things were going well for us at this time. I was doing contracting and my closest friend worked with me, while my wife looked after the home. Then my friend was killed in an accident at work. I had been sent to the builders' merchant for supplies and came back to find that my friend had slipped from the scaffolding and been killed instantly.

The next six months were really hard for me emotionally and psychologically and pushed me down really low. I had lost my good friend who was a lovely, happy man, the funniest man I have ever met. During this time my mum and dad helped me, encouraging me to try to move on and get on with my own life.

Then my dad became very ill and died. Almost immediately after this tragedy, my mum became ill and eight months later she, too, died. They were both in their early seventies. All this sadness built up in me and I was feeling very depressed.

Another craftsman and I were still employed by the contractor for whom we were working when my friend died. We always worked on big houses and gradually, over the next three months, I found that I was doing three men's work because the other two couldn't work; they, too, were very depressed and had psychological problems - post-traumatic stress, I suppose. After three months I was totally exhausted and said to the boss "I've had enough of this, I can't carry you two any longer, I'm leaving". I went home and I never looked back. I can only think that I had to shake off all connection with my friend's death before I could move on.

I had been worried about my friend's widow and spent a lot of time trying to help her through her grief. One day she asked me to take her to a medium, which I did. It was quite a moving experience although I can't remember much of what was said. Somehow I ended up with the medium's phone number and since then she has helped me from time to time. She also gave me the phone number of two ladies who are psychic and might be able to help me. I think it was sheer good luck that I went to see her - if I hadn't, I don't know what I would have done. At the time, I was emotionally drained and on the verge of a nervous breakdown.

For about six months I would go into the kitchen on my own after work and cook. I really enjoy cooking. It was the only way I could keep away from the kids because I was doing this thing where all day long I was grunting continuously - I used to do it at work and in the evenings too. I can only suppose that it was a symptom of my mental state - trying to cope with the loss of three people so close to me. I have since been told that this is not uncommon. The grunting is a noise that people make when their nerves are in a state of imbalance and it indicates the effort to concentrate. Occasionally, in crowded places (buses, the Underground, pubs, etc.) you see people twitching and grunting and this is a sign of extreme stress. Fortunately for me, it gradually stopped. My family thought I was going round the twist. My wife was concerned about the effect this would have on the children and so was I. I was worried too as the feeling was most unpleasant … I couldn't seem to be able to gain control of myself and felt very alone and vulnerable.

*****

Sadly, in many families, the death of a parent will cause friction between the children. This happened to us after my mother died. One of my brothers was extremely rude about her, which made me furious and I decided to have no further contact with him. Four weeks after her death, when I was still angry, I was cooking in the kitchen and my mother was suddenly standing there.

She said "Pink, please, you've got to do me this favour. I can't go, you're holding me back and I want to go to Dad now. You have to forgive someone for me so that I can go and you've got to mean it because otherwise you are going to keep me here and Dad's waiting for me and I want to go".

The only way I could do it was by writing so I wrote a letter saying in my head "I really mean this, I forgive you." Difficult though it was, I really managed to mean it and made a gigantic step which released my mother and, as a bonus, saved me from a nervous breakdown.

That day my life changed dramatically. I felt much stronger. I just felt fantastic and it seemed that I couldn't hate anybody any more and I actually felt good about forgiving. I was aware that one of the hardest things to do is to forgive someone who has wronged you. When I used to read in the papers that someone's child has been killed and that the parents forgive the murderer I used to think 'Imagine that, forgiving someone who has killed your child.'

Late one night soon after this event, my mum's and dad's spirits appeared and spoke to me in the kitchen. I had had a drink that evening, and I can't even remember exactly what they were saying, but they were telling me off and giving me advice. It was an amazing feeling being all back together for a while. I think that they must have come to give me some final advice before they went on their way for good to get on with what they have to do in the afterlife; I have never seen them since. The thing that I take comfort from is that, even though they had no religious beliefs, they were good people and I know that they are in Heaven and that I shall see them again. That is a real buzz for me.

Chapter Three

Dangerous Encounters

Only a few encounters with spirits have had a physical effect on me but these were truly terrifying because I knew I could be killed or at least made very ill. I was afraid of the risks in these situations and was hugely relieved when eventually I learned how to protect myself.

The first person I ever talked to about the spirits was my wife (about twenty years after we started living together) after a spirit tried to kill me. This was the most terrifying of the encounters I have had with ghosts; even now I get chills down my spine if I think about it. Although it is quite easy for me to help spirits to go on their way, some of them simply don't wish to go and have to be forced to do so. This was one of these.

At this point I was really happy - I was starting to get a name for myself and some very nice work was coming my way. I was just finishing work on the outside of a fairly large house, when a man walked up the drive and said that he had been watching me working and liked what I was doing.

He told me his name and that he lived across the road. He asked if I would go over and give him a price for painting his house.

I told him I would be there at four o'clock after I had finished work for the day. When I went over and saw that this was the largest house on the road I felt rather proud of myself! I looked at the work to be done and gave the owner the price, which he accepted. We agreed that I would start the following week.

The scaffolding arrived on time and I started work. I really loved working on this house, it was very rewarding: after about two months, the outside looked stunning. Every Friday my employer would pay me, shake my hand and tell me it looked fantastic! One Friday there were only two more days of work left and he asked me if I would do the inside as well and could I estimate how long it would take. I told him I thought it would probably take about six months.

I could hardly believe my luck when he said, "Great, it's yours."

Over the previous couple of months we had started to become friends so I was really looking forward to starting work on the inside the following week. At the weekend a television news bulletin reported on a horrible crash and named my employer as one of those killed. I was stunned and very sad.

On Monday I turned up for work not knowing what to expect or whether I would still be working there. There were three other people living in the house beside my employer - his fiancée, her sister and their mother. The sister met me at the front door and I could feel the huge weight of grief and shock in the house. After I had told her how sad I was and offered my sympathy, she said that the intention was to continue with the internal decorations as planned and that I would be dealing with her from now on. They did not want anything to be rushed, but everything should be done to the highest standard and she thought that, with what she wanted done, it would be more likely to take a year than the six months I had estimated. She asked if that would be a problem for me and I said it wouldn't. She told me that if I encountered any difficulties, I should let her mother know and she would contact her (the sister).

I used to get on really well with the mother and for the next two months she looked after me as if I were her son! We talked about Life and she made everything seem funny; it was a joy to go to work. Every Friday morning my wages were on the kitchen table in cash, along with a cup of tea and some toast and every Friday afternoon when I finished she would give me a little hug and a kiss and say "See you on Monday, have a lovely weekend."

Then, after a particularly good weekend, I arrived for work one Monday morning and the mother didn't come to the door. After a long wait the sister opened the door, apologised for keeping me waiting and told me, rather baldly, that her mother had died the night before. I was devastated because I had grown very fond of the mother.

The sister asked me, quite abruptly, to go upstairs when I had time and look at all the rooms and give her a rough idea of how long it would take. Towards the end of the week I went upstairs to look. There were five bedrooms, all en-suite. When I came to the mother's bedroom and opened the door it was quite dark because the curtains were drawn but, all of a sudden, it changed to black - deep black. I just stood there for a moment and then thought 'I have to go in and assess the paintwork' so I stepped into the room ... and suddenly something was trying to smother me with a cloak. I threw it off, stepped back out of the room and closed the door. My heart was beating very, very quickly and I was freezing cold; I didn't panic but just stood there on the landing. As I began to warm up, a voice said "Open the door for another look." I did and this time something tried to suck me into the middle of the room, so I closed the door and went downstairs, trying to understand what had happened. I was still very naïve and couldn't imagine what was about to happen to me.

The week went by really quickly. Everything was fine and I had a lovely weekend. When I arrived for work on Monday I saw the sister and she asked if everything was all right. I told her that everything was fine and she said she would see me at the end of the week.

I was now working in the house alone because the fiancée had started going to the gym every day and of course the sister was at work. There were four or five dogs in the house, all tiny Yorkshire terriers and all they did every day was yap - all day long. It didn't bother me because I had my radio going all the time.

One day, the sister had left for

work and there was no yapping at all - I was wondering whether the dogs had become sick, but surely they couldn't all be sick. I was painting the banister and all of a sudden a door upstairs, which was about four inches thick and weighed forty or fifty pounds (a fire door), slammed shut with great speed and force and a big black cloud which looked like smoke - from floor to ceiling and about six foot wide (which I now know to be a malign spirit), came down the stairs and said to me "Get out of my house" … and then he gave me a nasty electric shock!

Suddenly, I was standing by the door not really knowing how I got there or what was going on and he turned the amps up enough to make my lungs feel ready to burst. I used to be an electrician and, during my training, I once experienced a very nasty electric shock so I know what it feels like. I got out into the driveway thinking it would stop, but it didn't. He made me go all the way out to the road … and then he stopped.

I stood there for about five minutes and then told myself that I had imagined it, nothing had happened and I should get back inside the house and finish the job. So I walked back along the driveway. When I got to within about six feet of the house, I could feel him giving me electric shocks again from inside the door.

This time he was turning it up and I thought 'This is it, I've had it!'

I got back to the pavement and this time it really hurt. I thought 'He could kill me'.

I had been standing there for about ten minutes with my brush in one hand, hardening, and the paint pot in the other when the fiancée came back.

I walked up to the car and she asked if anything was wrong.

I said "No, I'm doing undercoating so I am getting a bit of air" and I thought 'Right, I'll let her go in first and see what happens'.

She walked right through the big black cloud as if it didn't exist but when I walked through it, it literally squeezed the breath out of me. What the malign spirit was doing to me was internal and wasn't showing on the outside.

As it was a Friday and I had just been paid, I said to her "I'm going to have an early day".

She said "OK, have a nice weekend". I got my keys and drove off.

It was my daughter's school sports day, so I went down to the playing fields, met my wife and told her that there was a really bad spirit at the house who was trying to kill me.

She said "What are you talking about - I don't know what you're on about".

I decided to ring the sister up and ask if I could meet her. She said she would be home at six and would meet me at the house. I told her I couldn't meet her there, that it was really important that I met her somewhere else. So we arranged to meet in a pub that I thought would be nice and quiet but unfortunately it was full of rowdies 'effing and blinding' in the background and I thought 'Oh no'.

Anyway I told her what had happened and she said "I'm quite intrigued - is it my mum?'

I told her it wasn't and she suggested that we go back to the house there and then.

I said "No, I can't, I've got to think about this and I have two friends who might be able to help me". So we left it at that.

Over the weekend I went to see the two ladies I mentioned in Chapter Two, friends of mine who are psychic, and I told them what had happened. They said they could help me and that we could go round there immediately. I told them that we couldn't go round, we had to ring first. But they told me to close my eyes as we were going there now. So I closed my eyes and found myself in the front room with the two ladies (I think this is a form of "virtual reality") and we looked into every room and I showed them the rooms I had already painted. Then we decided to go upstairs. Just before we got to the top, one of the women started groaning. I opened my eyes and saw that she was clutching her neck. When

I closed my eyes again I was back on the stairs with them. The black cloud was really dark, darker than it had been before - this spirit had a lot of power and had learnt how to use it.

When we got to the top of the stairs, the two ladies told me that they had found out that he had been a doctor. He had hanged himself and it had gone wrong. It took a long time for him to die and he was really, really angry and wanted to stay so that he could take out his pain and anger on whomever lived in his house.

We all opened our eyes at the same time and one of the ladies said "Yes, we can get rid of him. We'll come with you on Monday. We'll go up the stairs, I'll get him inside my body, he will speak and we'll find out what his problem is. Then we can send him on his way".

I rang the sister up and told her

what we were going to do, but she said "No, no. You come round on your own on Monday first and we'll talk it over".

When I arrived there on Monday at 8.30, the two sisters were waiting at the door for me. I'd obviously really scared them. We all walked upstairs together and when we got to the top of the stairs he was in the corner and just flew at me and started squashing me as he had done before. The pain was inside my body and they couldn't see it.

They said "Well, we can't see anything" and started walking down the stairs and the further they got from me, the more he was hurting me and I asked them both to wait for me.

When we got downstairs they said "We need to talk", so I said that we would have to go out onto the porch because otherwise he could hear us and would hurt me more and more.

They said "Look, we're not going to have some woman coming to our house, speaking like a man. If we can't see him and he's not bothering us, we're going to leave him upstairs. So we are going to have to get another painter and decorator, sorry".

What I really wanted to do, because they were such nice people, was to get him out of the house so that they would be safe but it would have been my biggest challenge yet and in any case they had said that they didn't want that.

It had been an interesting job. I used to get in on a Monday and they'd sit me down at the table and show me wallpaper and say "This is what we want in the library" or "This is what we want in the study. We don't want you to rush it, just take your time, have as much tea as you want". I'd think 'What a job I've got here, and it's only five minutes from my house.' It's a shame that it ended in the way that it did as I was learning a lot from the job.

I think this spirit has killed repeatedly over the years and will kill again. I gathered from my two friends that the doctor hanged himself at some point in the nineteen-thirties. Recently I drove past and the house was up for sale. My inkling is that over the years, whoever has owned the house has died. The spirit is doing it over and over again.

I've never come across anything else like it - something that could kill me. It was so physical; he took my lungs and I thought they would burst, but the first time I still had the courage to stand there and tell him to go away. I am quite proud of that, even though it didn't work! But now I have learned that I too have the power to send him away from me, just by pointing my finger at him. The whole experience was weird and still gives me shivers down my spine when I think about it.

I had had the job for six months and then I lost it. When I got home I told my wife and I said "Look, he will kill me".

My wife couldn't take it, we needed the money.

She said "If he doesn't kill you, I will!" I'll never forget the shock of hearing her say that.

I said that she didn't understand but she replied "I don't want all this stuff".

I lost the plot. Even in my mind I was thinking 'Am I imagining this - what is going on?'

I kept to myself in the kitchen so

that I could keep out of the kids' way. I didn't want to explain to them what was going on because I didn't want to scare them - I don't want my kids to be scared. Kids have vivid imaginations and I knew that, even if I told them it was OK, they would still be scared. I just thought 'I'm going mad, I'm losing the plot'. But I knew that everything that was happening to me - seeing spirits - was real and I feared that things would only get worse. There is nothing worse than being scared - for a grown man anyway.

*****

An American friend of mine has a house about five minutes from mine. He had had a decorator in who had made a real mess of the place so he asked me to redo it all - two months' work. The second I walked into the house the last owner but one, who had died of lung cancer in the top bedroom, gave me the pain of his lung cancer and followed me round for eight hours a day. He wouldn't say a word - wouldn't speak to me at all, just kept giving me this horrible pain. I even found it hard to breathe. If only I had known then how to point my finger and get rid of him as I do now!

I couldn't tell my friend because he'd have done a runner and he was obviously not troubled by the spirit. I worked in the house for eight weeks and it was a real chore to go in there. As I was leaving after I had completed the job I thought 'Thank God for that. You bastard, that really hurt'.

Six months later my friend had a flood and phoned and told me that they had had a flood. He asked me if I could come back and do the house. But I didn't go back - I wasn't having that again.

*****

I did a job in Sheen for a man who was having a house built at the end of Rosemary Terrace. I grew up near Rosemary Terrace - there used to be a short-cut to Mortlake station and there was a builder's yard there. There is a house next to where the builder's yard used to be and the man had an office built at the end of his garden. A cleaner lady I know, who has got me a lot of work for a number of people, was cleaning the house for the owners while I was painting their little office.

It's rather like a bungalow and I had nearly finished. All I had left to do was the loft hatch which was open - above it was all black. I'd just started painting it and ... heugh! A male spirit was there by the hatch (it really threw me because it was a brand new building) and, although I couldn't see him, he was feeding off me - draining my energy. I thought

'Oh no, not here'.

I walked out and was standing there wondering what was going on when the cleaner came out.

I said "You're never going to believe this: although this is a brand new building there's a guy up in the loft".

She said "Oh, didn't you know, this is part of an old burial ground. This is built on what used to be a cemetery".

I gritted my teeth and finished the job although it left me feeling utterly exhausted and a little ill. I had not yet learned how to defend myself against such attacks.

*****

My cleaner friend has a sister who had a flat in Putney which she used to rent out and it needed painting. One tenant had just moved out, so I had two weeks to get it done before the next tenants moved in. To reach it, there was the longest corridor I have ever walked down. It was like a road. I've never, ever, been down a corridor like this in a block of flats. It was on the third floor. As soon as I came out of the lift, this nasty spirit hit me - I couldn't see who, but it was there. It was invisible and although it didn't hurt me physically, it was draining my energy and it was horrible and very frightening. The flat that I was painting was at the end of the corridor. It was about 200 yards away. The spirit followed me all the way to the door. I can still remember, that first day, thinking 'Please don't come into the flat, please don't come into the flat'. That seemed like the longest walk I have ever had (to that door) and there were two locks to open when I got there which meant standing there for a minute at least and that was enough time for him to suck at my energy. It scared me.

I opened the door, closed it behind me and I thought 'He's outside - oh thank goodness, that's good isn't it? I can get on with my job'. All day I kept thinking about having to go out of the door - he's not nice and he started to follow me and drain my energy as soon as I left the flat … every time. I'd press the lift button, thinking 'Come on, come on' and feel enormous relief as I got in the lift. He couldn't get in the lift - he was confined to the long corridor.

On the second day I was thinking 'No, I don't like this. I'm getting weak'. I did not yet know how to get rid of the spirit. All I knew was that he was draining my energy and scaring me. My two youngest sons were nine and seven and it was the school holidays, so I said "You can come to work with me, I'll pay you five pounds each, I'll buy you breakfast and you can play with your wrestlers all day". Somehow I knew that when I had the kids with me, I wouldn't have a problem and nor would they. So I took them with me, gave them breakfast every day and they knew they were going to get a fiver and they were happy because they were bored at home and they could play with their WWF wrestlers.

On Friday, when I'd got the whole flat done, I said to them "Don't go mad in there". They had a massive bean bag with which they were playing and all of a sudden I heard "Oh no". They'd split the bean bag open and the whole room was full of millions of polystyrene 'beans'. So I thought, 'Right, get this cleared up and then I've just got the front door left to do'. I told the kids to watch telly or a video.

I was just finishing the door which

had a curtain over it covering a spy hole. It was the last hour of the job. My curiosity got the better of me and I looked through the spy hole to see what was in the corridor and there he was looking right back at me and sucking my energy through the door. I thought to myself 'my God what's happening to me?' As soon as I took my eye away from the spy hole he let go. I finished the door really quickly and said to my kids, "I've finished, come on. Let's go". I locked the door, held my kids' hands and walked to the lift with the ghost following us and still trying to suck my energy all the way to the lift door. I had known that he could really hurt me badly and wondered what would happen in the corridor but he could do no worse than take my energy because I had the kids with me - because of their innocence, double innocence. I was really frightened, however, and as the lift doors opened and closed shutting the ghost away, I thought 'I'll never go back there again'

*****

Nowadays some of my children are aware that I have encounters with spirits from time to time and have come to accept it even though they are not comfortable with it:

Recently one of my sons and I were working together on a job in the Kensington area and were going to catch the tube. As we walked toward the steps to the entrance at South Kensington I became conscious that someone, a spirit, had come out of the crowd on the pavement and was following me as we walked down the steps. He came closer and, as he did so, I began feeling colder and colder, even though it was one of the few hot days of the summer. By the time we reached the sliding doors at the edge of the platform he was right beside me. I was freezing, but very relieved when he didn't follow me onto the train. The chill must have shown as goose bumps on my arms or something because when we sat down my son said "Are you all right, Dad?" I told him that I was but that someone had been with me. He didn't say any more so I left it at that. I don't push the family to discuss these experiences because I do realise how strange it must be for them and I want to keep our relationships as relaxed as possible ... but it is hard for me.

Chapter Four

Controlling Healing Powers

My healing power was developing but I had not yet learned how to "ground" myself by placing my feet squarely on the floor so that the pain/illness I was helping people with passed through me rather than lingering in my body for a while (the same principle as a lightning conductor, I suppose). Because I didn't know how to prevent it in those early days, I used to take on the pain and illness of the people I healed and it would sometimes last for quite a long time, depending on how bad it was. Even since I learned how to avoid taking on the pain, it still happens when I don't 'ground' myself properly or when I don't have time to sit for a few minutes and allow my body to recover.

*****

The landlord of a pub we frequent was an ex-boxer and a really nice bloke. He'd done a lot for charity, which is great in my book. He had to take a great many pills a day just to keep him alive. He wasn't a drinker (he used to drink water), but he gradually got very ill with a kidney problem. I went in there one Sunday at lunchtime after I got back from watching my son play football. There were only a few people there, including the landlord's wife, who was a big woman (I'd even seen her knock blokes out!). She was sixty odd, but she was also very attractive. You could see that when she was young she must have been gorgeous.

Anyway she got hold of me, dragged me up the stairs and said "Quick, quick, he's gone". Because she used to work for so many charities she never had time to be around him constantly to make sure that he took his tablets.

She said "He's dead, he's dead, quick, do something!"

He was comatose, almost gone, and it was the first time I was put on the spot. Normally when I do healing it is just with one hand. Just this one time, because I thought he was almost dead, I put both hands on him and I could feel that he was nearly gone (I know when people are on their way out) and as I was doing it I thought 'I need help … please'. At once the room was full of people (spirits) - all men. I thought 'This is handy'.

It didn't scare me, not one bit, because I could feel they were all his friends. They all seemed to be boxers and were quite old. Anyway, by healing him with the extra power that both hands gave and the help of his spirit friends, all of a sudden he said

"Hello Pink, how are you doing?"

He sat up and said "Thanks for that. Cheers. Nice one." And his friends disappeared.

So I said "Are you all right now? OK mate?" and then I went downstairs and drank my pint. While I was finishing it, the landlord came into the bar and started chatting to people. His wife was on the phone in another room telling the family that he was dying and that they should come over as quickly as they could.

Then she came into the room and screamed "Oh! You're here, you're here!"

I need hardly say that she was amazed and very happy!

So I went home, had dinner, didn't tell anyone, kept it to myself; but the following day, Monday, I went to get out of bed and felt totally paralysed. I was so ill it was unbelievable. I was in bed for two whole days and the pain I had was really bad. This was because I'd done the healing with both hands instead of using one hand and allowing the pain to leave my body through the other one; I had taken all his pain into my own body. I didn't dare tell my wife because it cost me two days' pay - a lot of money! I have never used two hands for healing since.

*****

I don't tell anyone about most of the healing I do. People walk past me in the street and I can feel their pain. I passed somebody in Sainsbury's yesterday - an old woman. She had badly thinning hair and two big growths on her head and I couldn't help but look at them as I passed her. As I walked past I felt my knees grow weak and I felt the pain. It hurt me to think that I couldn't help her - you know … what if it was my granny? But obviously I can't help <u>all</u> the people <u>all</u> the time!

*****

I'd been healing a woman for five weeks. She had been diagnosed with terminal cancer and she had bad headaches. Her husband is a builder. I had met her about two years before and she was one of the kindest women I've ever known. They sent her into hospital straight away and operated immediately. The tumour was about the size of a tennis ball and they cut it out. In six weeks it grew back to the same size.

I asked her husband how she was and he said "We're just waiting for the day now Pink".

So I said to him "If your wife needs to speak to me, just let me know".

A few days later, she rang me and

the minute I was on the phone I felt I was helping her. I actually felt, even while we were speaking, that it started the ball rolling.

I said "I'll come and see you". We're talking about a woman who had been about size 10, and when I went round to see her ... there was this woman weighing maybe sixteen and a half stone. Her head was really big. You wouldn't even recognise her as the same woman. Her stomach was enormous. The steroids she was taking were doing this.

Three days after I'd been to see her she went and had her scan and the doctor said to her "I don't know how to account for this, but it's reduced in size". She was over the moon and so was her husband.

So I said "I'll come round again once a week and I'll be in your corner".

She said "I'd love that - if you'd be in my corner".

Every Thursday I went there and spent an hour talking and laughing with this woman who was dying and it was a laugh - the way she talked about life. She would get up at four just to hear the birds sing the 'dawn chorus'. She was somebody who loved life and didn't have a bad word to say against anybody.

When I was giving her healing, for about ten minutes, I could actually feel the force and my hand would not touch her head but hovered over her. I tried lowering my hand but something, like a cushion of air, prevented me from doing so. It was very, very warm and I thought 'Maybe I shouldn't touch her, maybe this is as far as I can go because I could catch it'. After I'd finished, she would fall asleep, but she loved the sleep and she enjoyed the relief of her headache going. She said she felt wonderful. For five weeks she was on steroids in reducing amounts to keep her balanced and I think she lost two stone. The doctors said that she could only come off the steroids slowly so each week she took a slightly lower dose.

After about two weeks she said "Guess what? I ran up the stairs".

I told her that I didn't think she should have done that but she laughed and said "Well, I wanted to and I did ... all the way up".

Her husband used to take her for walks down by the river every day and she kept having to stop. After a week or two she began to feel better and she would not stop talking - she could talk for England - I was there for an hour and a half one week and thoroughly enjoyed it. We made each other laugh a lot. We used to go for walks and after six weeks or so, she was striding along, whereas previously she had been very slow. I'm not saying I was the cause of her improvement. I'm not saying that at all. But she believed I was.

When I left her I used to get in the car and just sit for about half an hour. I couldn't go home straight away as I felt sick and ill. Afterwards, I'd drive for ten minutes or so and by the time I got home I felt better. But then I began to get scared because I started getting headaches - and I used to get neuralgia down the side of my face, which was very worrying. At first I didn't think it had anything to do with the healing I was giving to this woman, but then I thought, 'I've got to be careful here'. However, she now had the will to enjoy the time that was left to her and that made me feel good.

Sadly, she did die and, although I

couldn't heal her, I know that what little I <u>did</u> do made her happy and relieved some of her pain.

*****

A neighbour of mine has arthritis in his knee and, although I can't cure it, I can help by giving him healing to relieve the pain when it gets really bad. I work with him for five or ten minutes every now and then.

On one occasion something unexpected happened: I had been working for more than four months on a very big job and we had just finished the final, manic, week. This was a job where a number of the men I was working with had troubles of various kinds, common to people who work in the building trade. I had been holding 'clinics' during the lunch breaks! I had also been giving a series of sessions of healing to a child with very bad psoriasis. As a result of all the healing on top of the job itself, I was constantly feeling exhausted.

I was about to start a new job on the following day when I met my neighbour in the evening. He said that his knee was really giving him a lot of pain so I said that I would do something about it at the weekend when I would have more time and be more relaxed. We continued to chat for a while and I thought no more about it.

The following morning I woke up and went to start the new job. I couldn't believe it … my knee was in absolute agony. Climbing up and down ladders all day was dreadful. I thought 'This must be from my neighbour' so I phoned him and asked how his knee was. He told me it was fine - no pain at all. Without realising I was doing it, I had given him a healing session whilst we were chatting and, as often happens when

I'm not properly 'grounded', had taken on his pain. Being unaware that I was healing him, I had not been 'grounded' at the time so the pain lasted longer than usual and was more intense. Another lesson learned.

*****

So … I had discovered that my healing could happen at a distance (for example, on the phone) and equally that it could bring relief even if not a cure. However, I now had to consider how much damage it was doing to me and be very careful to develop controlling tactics such as 'grounding'.

Chapter Five

The Loneliness of the Healer

Sometimes the hurt I feel after giving healing is not physical but mental. When my family, or friends (not all of them!) ask what I have been doing during the day and I tell them about healing, their reaction is often one of rejection or anger. This can add to the hurt - and it is a very isolating feeling.

*****

My family and I were going on holiday to Turkey. On the way to the airport, my wife and kids asked me not to do any healing whilst we were on holiday, I told them not to worry - I was not planning to do so.

During our holiday, we'd gone out for the day and it was late when we got back to the hotel. The kids had gone up to bed because they were very tired. My wife and I were tired too but we just fancied a bottle of wine. The bar was open until about one in the morning so I said to her "Look, you go up, I'll get a bottle of wine and I'll join you shortly". Anyway … could I find anyone to serve me? The bar was open and I could probably have gone in there and helped myself, but I just don't do that, it's not me. So I walked around looking for a member of staff and eventually found the gardener. I'd seen him before, he would be at the hotel at seven in the morning, and he would still be there at one the following morning - he just worked all the time. I've never seen anybody work like that!

I said "Bottle of wine?" - I just about made myself understood. The usual bar staff could speak English, but his job didn't require much English. As well as ordering a bottle of wine, I asked "Can you open it for me?" and he gestured to say that his elbow was kaput. So I called him over, he put the bottle of wine down and I held his arm to try to heal it. He uttered some funny noises and I tried to make him understand that this was just between him and me and he wasn't to tell anyone. Afterwards, he opened the wine with no difficulty and gave it to me. I was glad to have been able to help. Although it is tiring, healing people gives me a warm feeling.

The next morning at breakfast we were being stared at by all the staff, even the waiters who brought us our breakfast were staring at us and the kids were obviously thinking 'There has got to be something wrong here …' The owner of the hotel is a woman whose husband is a surgeon at one of the hospitals. The surgeon happened to be sitting at the table next to ours and he came over and said to me: "Good morning. You are a very good doctor."

"What's he on about? What have you done?" asked my wife.

The surgeon said "I know what you did was really good."

The kids were saying "What are you doing? We're on holiday. Don't do it here Dad".

So we had a couple of days of the family having the hump with me because people were staring at us! Even on holiday this 'gift' was haunting me and yet, when the opportunity to help presented itself (the gardener) I couldn't refuse.

*****

At home one night, when my

daughter was about three, she came downstairs at about twelve o'clock, screaming with earache and in tears with the pain.

I said "Come over here" and put my hand on her ear. Her pain went away immediately.

She stopped crying, said "Thanks Dad" and ran back up to bed. I looked at my wife and the realisation hit home … to be able to do that for my kid was amazing!

My wife began to accept my ability after that, but she didn't want anyone to know. Nonetheless, people were beginning to find out about it.

*****

When the kids were young, almost every weekend would see us watching them play football. On one such occasion, we were watching my third son playing, when, all of a sudden, one of the other youngsters fell down and just lay there, screaming. People rushed onto the pitch with a stretcher and carried him off, still screaming, but nobody seemed to know any first aid. I could stand it no longer and got up. My wife said "No, not here, you'll embarrass our son" and I could see him gesturing at me from the pitch … but how could I leave the boy screaming when I knew I could help him?

Anyway, I went over to him and put my hand on him for a few minutes and whispered to him "I'm just a very good physio, OK?" When I took my hand away he stopped screaming and smiled at me and I went back to my seat. I wasn't very popular with my family for a while, but no-one had really taken any notice of me, so it was all right.

*****

One evening, after not having been out for months, we were going out for a meal and went in to a pub on the way. We saw a man there, a plasterer, who asked "Pink, someone said to me that you do healing?"

My wife said "What do you want?" She didn't like the bloke because he was always getting into fights.

He held up his hand, showing us that his fingers were tightly curled up. "If I trowel this ceiling tomorrow, I'll get paid for the whole job and I'm 'skint' - I really need the money".

My wife said "Go to Roehampton hospital, get it fixed, and leave us alone".

The guy was quite a hard nut, but I thought he was going to start crying. He said "Please Pink".

So I told my wife that we could go into the garden where nobody would see us. I took him out into the garden, sat down with him and I held his hand for about a minute. Even while I was holding his hand, he started wiggling his fingers and stretching and exercising them.

He said "Hell, Pink. That's amazing". When we went inside, he approached my wife, showed her his hand, and said, "Look at that!" She just looked at him.

*****

One morning, I was running late for a job in Farringdon, I hurriedly stopped to get cigarettes and a paper before catching a train. The woman in the paper shop was talking to another woman saying "I ill, I die, I go to hospital, I so ill …"

I had to catch the train and she was obviously going to be talking for another five to ten minutes, so I leaned over, grabbed her hand and held it (she didn't jump away or anything) and she just looked at me. I took my hand away, gave her the correct money, said "Ten Marlboro Lights, Mirror", picked up the items and rushed off to get my train.

Shortly afterwards, my wife rang me up and asked what time I was finishing that day. We arranged to meet at Sainsbury's in Kew at five o'clock. While we were doing the shopping, my head was still full of thoughts about work. At the checkout I heard a vaguely familiar voice saying "Your husband … he wonderful … he save me!"

As soon as I heard her, I thought 'Oh no! She's got two jobs. She works in the newsagents in the morning and then in Sainsbury's in the afternoon'.

My wife looked at me - "What are

you doing? You can't go round doing this to people! Who do you think you are?"

I said "I don't, I don't. It just happened. I was late for my train, I had to grab her hand to shut her up!"

Since then, the woman greets my wife every time she sees her. My wife is not too happy about this, given the reason; although she is a kind, caring person and is happy to help people who need it, like most people she is uncomfortable with what appears to be a 'magic' ability to help in a way most of us can't understand. The kids share her embarrassment.

*****

One of the worst reactions I ever got was after an encounter with a woman at work. I was painting a block of flats on my own - nice job. I was just about finished and was down on the ground floor.

The woman who owned the flat had just come back from the school run. I was painting the kitchen door and as she came in she started to cry. She put the kettle on and she had her back to me.

I asked her if there was anything wrong. She ignored me and carried on crying.

So I walked in with my paintbrush and my pot and I said "Are you all right?" She just kept crying. So I put the paint pot down and just held her hand - then she turned round to me and started smiling.

She said "Wow, I can't believe that".

I asked her what and she told me that she had been in so much pain that she was due to go into hospital on the following day to have her breasts reduced because of her back. She was an ex bunny-girl and she had big boobs.

She was over the moon, absolutely over the moon.

Later that day, as I was sitting in the kitchen, my wife asked, "So how did your day go?" I mentioned the woman.

I told her the story and at the end she turned around and said "Now look, this ex bunny-girl was crying in the kitchen and you went in, held her hand and her pain has gone, right? Do you think I was born yesterday? What sort of idiot do you take me for? Do you honestly think I believe that?"

*****

Finally, not everyone has a good reaction to my healing. Sometimes healing makes people jump. At eleven o'clock one night I went into the petrol station at the end of my road to get some cigarettes. The chap behind the counter looked totally exhausted. I knew that he worked very long hours as I had seen him there early in the morning, through the day and late at night.

I said "You look knackered." He admitted that he was very, very tired. So I asked him if he wanted to wake up.

He said "Of course I do".

I said "Give me your hand then".

I held his hand and he said "Yeuahh! Just leave it! No!"

I had thrown him a load of energy and I thought 'Oh well, it's your loss'.

Most people don't jump like that.

*****

That was about four years ago and there have been other such instances since, so I've now learnt not to say anything. So, whether it be because of embarrassing family or attempting to heal when it's not appreciated or even understood, the healer is, on the whole, alone and risks being left with no one with whom to talk about cases or experiences.

Chapter Six

The Word Spreads

Mark Westbrooke, a friend of mine who is a hairdresser, has sold me to England I think! I've known him for quite a few years - my wife gets her hair done at his salon.

One day, my wife and I were driving past his salon at about seven o'clock and he was standing outside. Elaine waved to him and he waved back.

He called "Pull over a minute", so I pulled over.

My wife asked how he was and he said "I haven't worked for six weeks and I'm the breadwinner in this place. If I don't work …" (He's got about eight staff in there - a lot of wages to pay out.)

He lifted up his jumper and he was wearing a surgical belt covering the whole of his chest and stomach - really thick.

My wife said "Go and give him twenty minutes' healing". (He's often said "People say you're ill Pink, you know, but I do believe". I don't think he truly believed until that day.)

I took him into his salon - there were only two or three people around. I gave him four or five minutes, that's all it was, without removing the belt. In fact, this was one of the most difficult healings I have ever given, partly because of the thickness of the surgical belt and partly because he didn't believe I could help (his pain lasted with me for several hours - as it often does if I have to combat disbelief). At the end of it, he got hold of his belt, threw it off and actually started dancing around the salon!

I said to him "If I were you, I wouldn't do that". But he went on doing a sort of ballet round his salon. He said "Pink, let me give you some money". I said "I don't need the money, this is for you, something for you". I know he does things for other people and he hasn't got a lot of money.

Later that evening, at nine o'clock, he rang me and said "Pink, you're not going to believe this, I feel fantastic! I've been cancelling these women for all these weeks and I have one really special client who pays a lot of money. She was going to a wedding and I had to cancel her. She's just rung me up and said 'You cancelled my appointment for doing my hair even though you knew how important this wedding was to me. Funnily enough, my daughter drove past your salon at ten past seven and you were jumping all over the place - literally jumping, like you were doing hurdles and whatever - and yet you cancelled my appointment and you knew how important it was to me'".

He told her what had been wrong and what happened and she said to him "Do you know what, that's the biggest load of rubbish I ever heard in my life and I will not be coming back to you ever again!" Then she put the phone down. But he's no longer in pain so he's happy.

Mark Westbrooke says:

"It's not often that you can use words like 'miracle', 'fantastic', 'unbelievable' or just 'wow' and really mean them, but just over five years ago I found one such occasion.

I woke up one summer's morning and thought about

the ridiculously busy day that lay ahead of me. But, hey, I seemed to feel fine so I threw my legs over the edge of the bed, all good so far, stood up and … sneezed. Something gave way in my back and agony ensued.

At this point I should mention that I have a history of bad backs having slipped a disc when I was young. It manifests itself by laying me up for one, two or, in extremes, five days at a time, but as long as I am careful it goes away … until the next awesome sneeze!

After a few moments of cursing - and, well to be honest, almost tears - I got myself together, put my clothes on and headed to the surgery. The doctor examined me and said I had partially slipped my disc again and should rest for four to six weeks. FOUR TO SIX WEEKS! I am self-employed, I run a busy salon.

Anyway, after ten days, I struggled into the salon for a staff meeting and training day - it was not a pleasant trip, I can tell you. When I got there the staff all made a fuss and commented on how old and crooked I looked (gotta love staff, always there to take the mickey.)

People who knew me kept popping their heads around the door and asking me if I was OK and asking when they could make an appointment etc … but the meeting was going well. Then a painter and decorator mate of mine came into the salon. Pinky (and yes, that is what we call him. I think it was because he went out one night to paint the town red and could only manage pink!) said "Got a bad back, I hear". I was a bit taken aback (pardon the pun) as I had no idea it was common knowledge. I confirmed that I had and then he said something strange …

"Want me to heal it for you Mark?"

Now I don't know about you, but the last thing I expect from a labourer, no matter how good they are at their job, is to be offered healing. I thought he was joking, but he wasn't.

He went on to tell me, and I forget the words he used, that he had a gift and could heal people and could fix me in ten minutes. I'm not being funny but I almost choked on my coffee. I do believe there are things in this world that cannot be explained, so I did not dismiss it and decided to give it a go.

He asked me to stand still and then ran his hand over my back without touching me and when he got to the damaged area he said, "That's the place isn't it?" And of course he was right. He then proceeded to 'heal' me by placing his hand on my back without any pressure. My back got very hot and after ten minutes he asked me to bend backwards. I told him there was no way I could as I could not even stand up straight. To my surprise I was already standing straight as I spoke those words. Pinky smiled.

Within seconds I could stand, bend and even jump. I was dumbfounded. I raced into the salon and jumped around like a child to the amazement of my staff and a random customer who had popped in to see how I was.

Now they say that every action has an opposite reaction and this is mine. Being so elated to be out of pain for the first time in ages, I ran out into the street and danced around like a fool, pointing at Pinky and telling all that he was a miracle worker. As I did this (and I found this out when she called me a couple of days later) a client who I had cancelled because of my chronic pain drove past. When she called, she was furious and explained that my then manager had called her to cancel explaining why but on the day of her appointment who did she see prancing around like a five year old, but me, Mark Westbrooke! I tried to explain about my miracle cure but she hung up on me and she has not been in the salon since, which is a shame. 'No pain, no gain' they say, but I will take no pain and one loss any day.

Pinky is amazing! He will

readily admit that his healing does not work on everyone; I guess you have to hold a little belief in the process. I do not believe it to be psychosomatic either because when I went to see my doctor later that day he was stunned by my recovery and still is today. My pain still comes back every now and then but to a much lesser degree and less frequently.

I will be forever grateful to a friend called Pinky".

*****

Mark has been telling all sorts of people about me. So for the last year I've had people just flying at me - from all directions.

One of them was a man who could

hardly walk. He's an actor and part-time decorator (I'd never heard of that combination before). He asked if he could come to my house and I told him he couldn't but that I'd meet him at my local pub at five to twelve on Sunday when there would be no-one there. I said I would give him ten minutes. So he said "OK, I'll be wearing a blue jumper".

I'd meant to tell him not to have a drink but when I got there at twelve he was sitting outside with a bottle of Bud. He'd drunk a bit of it so I said "I meant to tell you not to have a drink yet." He said that he had only had a little and offered to buy me a drink. I asked for a sparkling mineral water and he said he would go and get it. He walked to the bar (it's quite a distance) and I saw that he was walking completely doubled up. I looked at him from behind and thought 'This is really going to hurt me' (and it did!). I knew it would because he was literally almost on his knees.

The manager was at the bar when he got there and he served him. There were two other girls present (bar staff) but nobody else was in there. My client gave me the mineral water. We went down to the end of the bar and he leaned on the bar and I did ten minutes on the middle of his back. Then I did five minutes on the area at the base of his spine. So … there he was with me behind him and I was shaking as I sometimes do when I'm healing. The manager came over, looked at this chap bent over and asked if there was a problem.

My 'client' said "Well, can I tell you in a minute?"

Then the manager looked at me and said "Have you got a problem?"

"No", came my reply.

After I'd done his fifteen minutes and stopped, my client walked back along the bar and as he walked he straightened up. This man hadn't been able to put his shoes on for three months. First of all he did ten press-ups off the bar - straight off. The manager was watching this from the other end of the bar. The pub has one door in and one door out and the guy started jogging out of one door and in at the other and after he had gone round three times I said "Look, I think you should calm down now". He thanked me and gave me fifty pounds which was very kind of him.

*****

Another one of Mark's "referrals" is a woman who lives on Kew Green. He asked if I could go and see her and I said that I would on the following Sunday. When I arrived, I asked what her problem was and she said "Well I can't swing my golf clubs, I can't play tennis and I miss skiing and they are the three passions in my life".

I spent five to ten minutes and she paid me £20 which I did not expect. Anyway she rang me up the following day and she said "I've just got to tell you that I very felt sick immediately after you left, but today I got up, I've played a game of tennis, a round of golf, and I've just bought myself some skis and I'm going skiing tomorrow, how about that?" I said "Well done" and she thanked me and that was it. It was a problem with her shoulder.

*****

Mark, my friendly hairdresser, phoned me one day and asked where I was as a friend of his had a back problem and couldn't walk. As it happened, I was just round the corner.

I said that his friend couldn't come into the house because there were people there, so I arranged to meet him outside the church just down the road. When he arrived he really struggled to get out of his car. This turned out to be another episode where the pain which transferred to me lasted a long time - nine hours this time and it really hurt. It was also one of the experiences which taught me the most. I learned about extra problems which had not been mentioned (in his case, his knees) and to be aware of them.

I proposed a walk into the church grounds.

For him it seemed more like a crawl, so I just gave him healing on his back and while I was doing it, my knee was killing me - this one really hurt me. So I bent down and put my hand on his knee and said "Why didn't you tell me about your knee?"

He said "I didn't tell you because I wanted my back pain to go". When he got up, we walked to his car and he got in with no effort.

He said "Thanks mate, I can't believe it, I've got absolutely no problem now".

He was obviously pleased with the result as he sent his account of what happened:

Mark Weston writes his story:

I met Pinky a couple of years ago when I was thirty-four.

I am no stranger to pain and injuries as I have been a personal fitness trainer for sixteen years, qualified for treating many of my clients' ailments and am always party to the various rehabilitation programmes they undertake for occasional back, knee and stiff shoulder pains. My own legacy of intensive sports, and particularly ten years of Judo training, had left me with very worn cartilage in my knees, but, more seriously, a compound disc problem in my back which had increased in its intensity over the preceding months to leave me with searing electric-like sciatic pains up and down my lower back, the back of my legs and my arms.

The problem had been getting worse and on this particular day was so bad upon waking, that I was virtually unable to move my arm sufficiently to clean my teeth or eat anything and barely able to lift my foot high enough to climb the stairs. I could manage a foetal position to lie in, or hunched in a chair, but could only stand or shuffle about in a Neanderthal-like forty-five degree angle - and that with gritted teeth. I had been brought up with parents who had a very British attitude towards pain, that taught that most niggles could be cured with a strong cup of tea and a biscuit or a brisk walk. Indeed, I had been to the doctor's only twice in my life prior to that, once when I was born (unavoidable) and once with a broken arm from a Judo fight, and that was under protest. The idea of spending two hours in A&E just to receive some painkillers and exercises that I already knew was not high on my agenda and it meant that I opted instead just to lie there.

However, later that day a good friend who had heard about the situation contacted me, and he put me in touch with Pinky and as I was finding it harder to 'just be brave', let alone get to the biscuit tin, I drove to see him. Surprisingly, sitting in the car was actually less painful, as I was sitting down, even though getting in and out of the car took an age.

I was a little taken aback by his appearance as he approached. My preconceptions didn't quite stretch to the robed guru or bearded, saintly mystic that my friend had indicated that he was, but the wiry man in plasterer's overalls, complete with fresh plaster and paint on him, who appeared, was certainly not what I had expected.

(*Well, I* **was** *in the middle of a working day!*)

He seemed at first to be a little nervous of the situation, occasionally avoiding eye contact but, with hindsight, I realised that doing what he does, he must be confronted with any number of sceptics and detractors. It is not surprising that he would be as wary of me as I potentially would be of him and as we met, he was indeed watching me carefully. That said, I do remember thinking that he had a very calming aura about him. He spoke softly and slowly and did make me feel at ease very quickly. I am glad that he appeared as he did, as dressed up in some red mystical garb wouldn't have endeared him to me so immediately.

He asked briefly what the problem was but it was obvious to anyone what I was going through. He stood behind my left shoulder and began to trace patterns, gently touching the area on my lower back occasionally and, bizarrely enough, mumbling the odd word to some unseen person or chuckling slightly to himself. At one point I'm sure I heard him say, "Yes, I know" to someone.

After four or five minutes nothing seemed to be happening and, as much as I really wanted this chap to be the miracle worker that he was purported to be, I was getting desperate. At that point his mobile rang and, apologising profusely, he said he really needed to take the call. He stepped away a few yards but before he spoke to the caller, he called over, gesturing at my back,

"If it's working, Mark, your back should be warm" he said.

I must confess that at this point a few warm words were passing through my head to say to him upon his return but, as I put my hand on my back as he was suggesting, it was not quite my back that was warm - but my t-shirt! It was as if it had just been ironed a few seconds earlier. There was a definite and tangible warmth to the area on my clothes.

I should also explain at this point that I am certainly not the sceptic in dealing with such things and have more than a passing interest in all things spiritual, mystical and so on. I desperately wanted this to work, not only for the obvious relief from pain but also for my own personal reasons and theories concerning such talents. But, up to that point, despite my open-minded willingness for it to work, it quite simply wasn't working. But the warm t-shirt instantly changed that. Also, I am very aware of the power of suggestion and of the abilities of hypnotists and of NLP practitioners in their work as I have friends who work with such skills and I deal with them on a daily basis. I am confident about the possible consequences of any tricks that he could have played and I knew this was no suggestion, conventional hypnotism or street magic trick.

He returned from his phone call and we were both changed. He was smiling with his very engaging eyes and was more confident, not for himself but for me.

"Now you believe me, don't you?" he said, "you *really* believe me. You have to trust this will work or it won't."

The patterns and the mumbling continued for a few more minutes and, to my amazement, I literally felt the pain begin to 'gather up' from the various areas in my buttocks, middle back and arms and shrink to an area in my right hip. The pain was still intense and if anything was stronger, but it was the size of my palm, on my lower right hip-bone - which made little sense to my physiological mind, as there was no muscle structure there that had been affected before. I talked him through what I was feeling and Pinky responded by making pulling movements as if he was pulling a rope out of that exact point. He began to say, over and over, "Come on, get out! Get out!"

Within seven or eight minutes I was standing up straight and, incredibly, was lifting my knees up higher than my belt in a marching movement. I gingerly began to twist from the waist, bend forward and back a little and raise my arms above my head - all of which was possible with a lot less pain and all of which was definitely not possible twenty minutes earlier.

It was simply amazing. I had to know more about

how he did it and, for my own reasons, asked him a stack of questions, all of which he answered. Then, to add further to my astonishment, Pinky questioned me about someone in my life about whom I was holding bad feelings. I confirmed this by telling him of a recent breakup of a serious relationship and how I probably still harbour resentment. He recommended that, in order to help the healing process, I contact this person immediately to forgive her and to clear the air. This aspect of the treatment was the most unusual to me. I wasn't sure whether it was *Reiki* healing, spiritual healing or any other faith-based talent - or whatever - that he had used on me, but I do know that I believed in it and it worked. However, the connection between my *physical* sciatic pain and the emotional pain that I had gone through required a whole different set of understandings and beliefs.

Getting back into my car, I telephoned my dad straight away to tell him. I simply had to tell someone … but as I looked in the mirror I saw the departing figure of Pinky was now bending over in the road, much as I had done for the previous few days. When I went over to him and questioned him about this he explained that he had "taken on" my pain. I had heard of this aspect of the process before and sceptics would say that it was for show … but what wasn't in the script was when he said, "Wow, you didn't tell me about your bloody knees!" I certainly hadn't. I had not mentioned at any point about my consistent knee ache from my cartilage problems. Pinky most definitely had. He explained that now he was experiencing both the knee and the back pain at one time and he even told me which knee was the worst and the exact type of pain I was feeling. I felt terrible for apparently unloading this onto him but he assured me that it would pass in a few minutes.

We said our farewells and

I drove home, still reeling from the experience. I immediately called my ex-girlfriend to explain that I had no bad feelings and did not hate her for the breakup. We became instant friends again and, although we didn't get back together, we remain great friends to this day and I never again felt the emotional hurt from that breakup.

The next day, I drove eighty miles to Woburn Abbey, to see the singer Neil Diamond in concert, meeting there with my parents, uncle and aunt. Up to the previous day there was no chance that I could go at all as the drive and two hours in a seat would have killed me. I arrived a little late for the show and parked some eight hundred yards from the stage area and so I ran, *actually ran,* to my seat. I cannot emphasize enough the stark contrast between the 'me' from the previous three weeks, where getting dressed was a twenty minute affair, to the 'me' jogging through eight hundred yards of fields to see Mr Diamond sing 'Forever in Blue Jeans'.

Within three more days the pain had all but subsided and, several years on, I have never suffered again with any serious back pain. I will always be grateful to that very unusual and gifted person, Pinky, and will never hesitate to recommend him.

Despite Pinky's own insistence that he is not as such the healer and only acts as a channel to open up the pathways between the patient and the 'healers' and good energies, I feel that what happened that day was as close to a miracle as I will ever see. He is a very special man.

Chapter Seven

Challenges … and Perks

People ask me how and why I began healing and what it feels like when I do it. I'm not really sure, but I think it was an instinct that told me to put my hand on someone in pain for a few minutes. When I found that it helped, I couldn't stop … how could I not do it when I know that I can help people in pain? It's not easy to describe how I feel when I am healing; usually I feel very calm and focused and I can sense if I need to move my hand to a place where the problem is more intense. I can feel power flowing through me and it is a good, warm feeling. When I am trying to draw away pain it is a bit different: sometimes it is a real effort, particularly if the person is resistant, and it really drains me. If I don't 'ground' myself by putting my feet squarely on the ground and sit for a while afterwards to let my body recover, that is when the pain stays with me for quite a while (they are right when they say "It pays to go through the proper procedures"!)

There are so many people who need help, I can feel them all around me, but I have had to learn that I can't help them all. When I first started healing I wasn't mature enough to realise that I should be disciplined about it and I drained myself of energy and started to look older very quickly - it actually added about ten years to my appearance. I wish I had known then what I know now: that it is important to 'ground' yourself so that the ill effects drain away out of your body, but I didn't know and have paid the price. So if you feel that you, too, can heal … bear in mind that there is a price to pay if you don't treat your own body too. It could have taken over my life but now I know that there are times when I just have to say "no" - because somehow I know it won't work.

At first, when I didn't know about 'grounding' myself, it was hit and miss whether I took on the pain or it went through me and away. I have already told about some of the worst pain I took on; luckily, now I don't often have it.

*****

One Sunday lunchtime after football, I was surprised to see a friend of mine in the pub as he used to go down to his caravan every weekend. He was a painter, in his sixties, a real character, whose company I very much enjoyed as he made me laugh a lot.

He was coughing, every minute or

so, and told me he had been bringing up lumps of blood and mucus all weekend. He asked me if I could do anything about it.

I said "I tell you what, I don't know if I can but I'll try. But we must make a deal. I'll try and help you, but I can't cure you so you <u>must</u> go to the doctor first thing in the morning - you have to promise me that".

It was obvious that he should have gone to the doctor many months before and, although I knew I could alleviate his symptoms to some extent, I also knew that I couldn't cure him.

He promised he would, so I took him into the toilet in the pub and spent five to ten minutes on his stomach and he stopped coughing. He stopped coughing just like that - he even lit up a fag.

The following week, I went into the pub and he was there with his son, who I knew - I had worked with him once when he was an apprentice on a building site.

His father said "Pink, do my son a favour will you? His elbow's completely gone - he knocked it at work, he can't even lift his pint".

I didn't bother taking him to the loo, I just put my hand on the bar under his elbow and in about thirty seconds he said "I can lift my pint now, cheers Pink".

I asked my friend how he had got on at the doctor's.

He said "I'm fine now, I haven't coughed since last week so I didn't go".

I was very concerned and told him he really should go to the doctor, that we had a deal and it was very important that he did go, but he wouldn't. Sadly, he died; but he lasted another eighteen months. Whether he died because he didn't go to the doctor or whether he would have died anyway I don't know, but I feel that it's very important to advise consulting a doctor.

*****

I used to go to football with another friend for about ten years - I would see him every Sunday along with the same group of parents. He had been a brick layer, but had constant back pain and had been told that his spine was very badly damaged. He was the manager of the football team. We started getting friendly again. He's a huge man and he's Chelsea mad.

He used to walk all hunched over and with great difficulty and I often asked him to let me have a go at his back and he would say "No, no, no, I don't want any of that".

Eventually the need to help was overwhelming! On one particular Sunday, he had told me that he was booked to have a plate put in his spine in about three weeks' time. He was hobbling across the street and I gave him some healing right there! He was clearly very embarrassed. There were cars and people going past and I made him stand there in the middle of the street for about ten minutes while I healed him. (Imagine if my wife and kids had been with me!)

He went home and said to his wife "This is the first time I've been pain-free in ten years".

She said "He's been offering to do it for you for years".

About a year later he had a lump on his arm and I put my hand on it and it went. He's a builder and has a good heart - would do anything for you. When he saw that lump go down … that was it, now he believes this can happen.

*****

I meet my builder friends on a Friday and one of them, a window cleaner, is a real pain when he's had a drink and he just likes an argument. One Friday he got into discussing religion with another mate of mine. I wasn't really listening but after half an hour of arguing, my mate said "I'm going to throw him over to you Pink, all right?'

So then the guy said to me "Go on then, what's God? What's He ever done? Go on, you tell me, you prove to me what God has ever done".

He went on and on and in the end I said "Look I've had enough, I don't want to talk to you about it any more.

Just stop it now".

The following Friday the same bunch of builders was over in the corner and I thought 'To hell with it, I'll go and sit with another group'. But the big builder caught my eye and he called me over.

So I went over to him and said "What's the matter?"

He said "Pink, do us a favour, can you heal his hand?"

It was the window cleaner, the cantankerous chap who keeps getting into arguments. I said "What's the matter with your hand?"

He showed me his hand and there was a lump the size of a golf ball poking out of his palm (he obviously couldn't hold his squeegee) and he said "Can you do anything for it?"

Now this is the guy who had been

giving me all the nonsense the week before. I said "Yeah, I can do your hand". I held his hand for about a minute and then I let go.

The first thing he said to me was "Bloody hell, that's bloody magic."

I said "Is that what you think? Do you think it's magic?"

"Yeah. That's bloody magic."

I said "Well you ponder on that, because if you think it's magic, then you've got a problem".

For a few months after that he wasn't cantankerous any more, he'd calmed down - something had hit home and that, for me, was a little treat because I had proved to him that there is something there, perhaps even changed his mind about God. Incidents such as this bring a huge satisfaction because someone's outlook has changed and without that the healing wouldn't happen.

*****

Just after we came back from holiday, my car, a Volvo, broke down and had to be scrapped. For four weeks I carried my ladders and all my tools to the job I was doing in Sheen and walked home again.

The builder I was working for at the time, asked "Will you do me a favour? Will you do a job for me this weekend? It'll just take you Saturday and Sunday and it'll be done - it's the outside of a house".

I thought 'I've got to catch up financially and that will help a lot.' So I agreed. I turned up for the job, met the couple, nice people, and I got started on the job. After half a day the man came out and said "Do you know I've been watching you doing a really, good job. Your prep's really good".

So I thanked him.

Late in the afternoon I had to go into one of the rooms and he was there working on his computer. I had to lean out of the window and I was busy painting when he said "Are you definitely going to be here on Sunday?" I said that I would be because I had to go to another job on Monday.

He said "Well, my wife's going to church at eleven and I'm going to watch my friends play tennis. Do you need to get in?"

I said, "No, that's not a problem. So you're not playing tennis then?"

"No, I haven't played tennis for about four years".

I looked at him and he had a tic in his eye, which told me that he had probably had a slight stroke. Now this guy's only in his forties and he's a big man. He was sitting down and he said "My knees are gone and my back's gone".

He was facing me and I was busy painting. I kept looking at him and thought 'That stroke's at least four years old'. You know when you see someone with just a little tiny tic? ...

He said "I used to love playing tennis but I just don't play any more".

So I put my pot and my brush down and I put my hand on his knees and I looked up and just as I did that his wife walked past in the corridor to go to another room, and there's me in my overalls bent over her husband's lap … so she stopped. She came back and walked into the room, said "Oh" and walked out - goodness knows what she was thinking!

Then I said to him "Can you stand

up?" He stood up.

I laid my hand on him again and he said "Oh. What can I say?" I told him he didn't have to say anything. Then he said "I can't believe this" and started strutting around.

I told him that I had to go and he said "OK" and sat back down. He was clearly too stunned to discuss what had happened.

The following morning I arrived for work and, even though it was cold, he was getting into his car in a pair of shorts and trainers with his tennis racquet in his hand. He said "I'm off! I'm off to play tennis. Thanks very much". I said "That's OK".

At the end of the day I just went off because the builder was going to pay me on Monday so I didn't need to see the clients.

On Monday, because I was

working in the next road, I just had to get my ladders off the scaffolding so I thought, 'I won't wake them up, I'll just be very quiet'. So I got my ladders down off the scaffolding and just as I got them down I knocked the scaffolding and there was a little 'clunk' noise. Anyway, I was part of the way up the road with my ladders when the guy came running up.

He said "Pink, I just don't know what to say. Did you say to me that you walked here and you walked home?"

I told him I did. My car had broken down for the final time and had had to be scrapped so I was saving to buy a replacement.

"You have no wheels?"

"No".

"Well, I've got two cars, do you want one? The spare car's got a year's

MoT, a year's tax and it's immaculate. Here are the keys. It's parked up that road there. If you like it, go and get it. And if you want it, come and see me tonight and I'll give you the documents"

I walked up the road, found the car, got in and, even though it's only a small car, I could just get my ladders in it. Brilliant. So I went round there that night after work and he handed me all the documents. He even included a year's AA breakdown insurance.

I said "That's really kind of you".

He told me that it was actually his wife's car but they didn't really need two vehicles. His wife was thrilled because he was playing tennis and she'd seen him in so much pain for so long.

Then I said to his wife "That really

is very kind of you".

She replied "Listen, we are over the moon. Thank you, thank you very much. You will look after my little car won't you?" I promised I would and she said "I'm happy then".

So now I was driving around in the car and the builder went to see if the job had been completed to the client's satisfaction and the man told him what I'd done and that he'd given me a car. There was no problem so far as the builder was concerned because I didn't have a car and they know I've got to get my tools around. Now it's a big joke to all the builders ... "Here comes Pinky, what's he going to get from the next job?"

But it does show how significant it is for people when the burden's lifted and it is really gratifying to be rewarded on some occasions. Although I neither expect nor ask for any recompense - what a lovely feeling when it happens!

*****

The next job was for a really nice couple who'd been trying for a baby through IVF for a long, long time. The wife had been telling me about it over coffee one morning, so I held her hand for a while.

I don't know why it was but I just got on well with this woman. We used to talk at lunchtime about spirits and angels. Then one day I felt something different in the house. It was a nice feeling, it was good. She came up to me and I looked at her and I could see little pixies - tiny, tiny ones, flying round her, and I thought 'Blimey, she's pregnant'. She asked me if I was ok and I told her I was fine. I was looking away because I knew, and I couldn't help staring at the pixies.

She said "Is there a problem? Have I done something to upset you?"

I kept looking away and said "No, no everything's fine".

When she asked again if there was a problem, I just grinned.

She said "Come on, tell me".

"You're pregnant".

"Oh wow!" she shouted, and she started running around.

I said that I shouldn't really have told her and asked her not to tell her husband because he is a non-believer. She told me that she was going for a scan in a week's time.

So for a whole week I was trying not to laugh or smile - trying to keep a straight face. I told my wife and she said "You shouldn't have told her, you could be in big trouble here."

The following week, the woman went for a scan and when she came back she said "I'm pregnant - I know it's down to you".

"Well if you believe that, I believe that".

Now her daughter is not quite three years old. I've been back there again doing some more painting, and seeing the parents and their the little girl so happy gives me a lot of pleasure.

*****

Not all the healing I do is just physical, often things which are in peoples' minds or stress and tension make them suffer. Sometimes I just talk to them and it helps; when I see the stress going away it makes me feel good too!

Chapter Eight

Spirits in Limbo

I suppose you could say that, when I send spirits who are stuck here on their way that too is a sort of healing. Some are still here because they do not realise they have died. Presumably their passing was so peaceful that they are unaware that they are no longer attached to their bodies and these spirits need to be told that they should move on and follow the light to the next stage of existence.

Some spirits simply don't know how to proceed and these need to be shown where the light is and told to follow it.

Others are being held here by their loved ones being unable to 'let go'. In these cases it is those who remain behind who have to be shown very gently that it is in the best interest of the dear departed and, indeed, of themselves that they say 'goodbye' and allow their loved ones to go and find peace.

I think that, out of all the experiences of this type that I have had, this is the one that left me with the best feeling:

About ten years ago I used to go to the local swimming baths every Sunday with my brother Greg and the kids. We used to spend our time in the kiddies' pool - we never went into the big pool. One Sunday I said to Greg "I've got to have a swim". So he said I should go ahead while he looked after the kids.

I dived in and immediately there was a huge flash of light and I felt as if I'd been hit by lightning. A ten-year-old boy's spirit appeared right in front of my face, looking very scared and unhappy, and I panicked - quite apart from the shock, I couldn't believe there could be a ghost stuck in a swimming pool. I swam to a rope between the lanes and I hung on to it. I was gasping and breathing really quickly because I thought I might drown.

The guard spotted me from the seat and asked me if I was all right. I gasped again and said "Yes, thanks".

Not wanting to repeat the experience, I got out and told my brother about it. At first he thought I was joking but I assured him I wasn't and he could see that I was pretty shaken, so we cut the swimming session short and went home.

I didn't go swimming for three months after that and the kids kept saying "What's the problem? Why aren't we going swimming?" They missed it so much.

The boy I had seen, who had drowned in the swimming pool, was obviously stuck, - in limbo. There are people who do rescue work, but I did not know who to contact about it.

My wife suggested that I should attempt to do it myself and told me that she would come with me. I agreed to try it. She seemed to have changed her attitude, possibly because the kids were missing their visits to the swimming pool.

We went to the baths and got into the water at the shallow end. I said to her "Don't let go of my hand, because I can only hold my breath for a minute and I don't know what's going to happen".

So I held my breath and put my head under the water ... the flash of lightning came again and he was there in my face, still looking scared, and I talked to him through my mind. I knew he could read my thoughts and I said to him "I'm not the light you are looking for but if you turn round there's another, there's one waiting for you right there. Your friends are there and your family, all people who love you, they want you to go to that light. If you look round, you are going to see the light".

I thought the fear might go from his expression but it didn't. He just turned round and he didn't swim, he just seemed to glide through the water … and then he disappeared. And that was that. And I came up and I cried and so did my wife. That meant something to me. She asked if he had gone and I said "Yes".

*****

I'd been doing my second job with a builder, when he rang me up and

147

said "We've got a month to get this house done. The people who have bought it have gone to America and we've got electricians, plumbers and painters booked and we've got four weeks to get it done, finished and out, so that the new people can move in".

After two days of working on this job, I started hearing wind chimes and I thought 'Oh, now they sound nice.' There were two gardens - one big one leading to a smaller one which was very overgrown. The following day the chimes were all I could hear, even though I had the radio going, which I thought was rather strange.

At lunchtime I went out, found the chimes and climbed up the tree from which they were hanging and took them down. I thought that obviously the people who have bought the house didn't know they are there because the gardeners had only just started cutting through all the overgrowth.

I put the chimes in a bag, took them home and I said to my wife "You are going to like these". I have a big Eucalyptus tree in my garden which I planted when we first moved in and it's now about twenty feet tall, so I went into the garden and hung them on a branch. For the next three weeks after that I had nothing but trouble. Everything was going wrong - work, family stuff, etc. At the end of this time, the job was all but finished. My third boy was studying for his GCSEs at the time. He woke me up at two in the morning and said "Look Dad, I've had enough. Will you just come and listen to this now. It's been going on for three weeks". He was obviously very scared.

We went to his bedroom, leaned out of the window and there was the sound of a big ball being bounced on the concrete. It made a "bomp, bomp, bomp, bomp" sound.

He said "Dad, this has been going on for three weeks until six in the morning".

"Why didn't you tell me?"

"Because I thought it might stop".

So I went down to the garden and I said (I couldn't see the ball, just hear it) "Now just go away". It stopped and I went upstairs and said to my son "It's gone now". But then in the morning I had a strong feeling that something was wrong here and, for some reason I can't explain, I knew it was the chimes. I went back into the garden and climbed up the tree, put them in a carrier bag and said to my wife "There's something wrong with the chimes. I don't know what's going on but there's something wrong".

I took the chimes and went to see my psychic school friend, Scatty, and told her what had happened. She touched the chimes and was silent for a little while then said "You've done something bad. You've taken the chimes from the house in which a little girl who was really badly abused used to live. The chimes and the ball were all she had. She was actually killed eventually. You've got to take them back and put them where you found them. She will meet you there and she's going to tell you who killed her. And be careful of the well". I didn't know what she meant by that - there was no well in the garden.

So then I had to ring the builder up because the people had just moved in. I told him everything and fortunately he believed me.

He said "Right. I can get the keys in two days' time because we've still got the contract to do the gardening. I'll meet you there in two days with the keys".

When I met him there, he gave me the keys and said "Drop them off at my house, I'm not staying".

I went up to the door and said "I'm just attending to something in your garden very quickly, is that OK?" They said it was. So I let myself in through the side gate and went through the main garden and into the other tiny little garden (like a secret garden) and there was the tree. I climbed the tree, put the chimes back on the branch from which I'd taken them and I came down and sat under the tree and waited. In a few moments a girl appeared in front of me. She was wearing a light green patterned dress with long sleeves and frills round the hem and neck. I imagine she was about eleven or twelve, no more than that.

I said "Is there anything you want to tell me?" "No, I want you to help me to go, right now. I want to go right this second".

So I said "Well if you turn round you'll find your light and you just go to that". So she turned round and she walked about ten feet and then just disappeared.

The builder had told me that if she told me who killed her I would have to go to the police. I had been getting worried about that, so I was glad that she didn't tell me and that she just wanted to go. It actually felt good - just being under that tree. My heart felt wonderful, everything felt nice around me - just for a couple of minutes. It was an unforgettable feeling.

*****

Two or three years later I was working in a very old house in Surbiton. It was a lovely old house and I was papering one of the rooms with very expensive and attractive wallpaper. Because the floors and ceilings were a bit wavy and the paper was patterned it was difficult to get the pattern to match and I kept running out of paper. It just seemed that it wouldn't go right. In the kitchen there was a well, covered in thick glass which you could walk over and see into its depths. I could feel that there was a presence there and didn't go near it.

One evening I met Scatty in the pub. I hadn't seen her for some time, and we were chatting. I told her about the well and she suddenly said that there was a little black girl whose parents had been servants in the house. She had had a pet dog and it had been thrown down the well so she was still there, grieving for the dog. She was a mischievous little girl and loved playing tricks and she had recognised that I could help her and had been making the room harder to paper than it should have been in order to stop me finishing the job and going away.

Scatty said that I should talk to her and send her on her way but I asked her if she would do it. She agreed to meet me there after work one evening and I would finish the papering while she sent the little girl on her way. So we did that and the little girl was reunited with her beloved dog and they both walked to the light and went on their way to where her family was waiting for them.

Chapter Nine

Mediation

There have been a few occasions when spirits who have been stuck because their loved ones were holding them here have actually used my body to make their wishes known to their families. Others stay because they feel they can still do something to help.

*****

A friend of mine is a posh builder who does work for a lot of very rich people, most of them millionaires - all of them nice people. One of his clients is a chap in the city who is doing really, really well. He had just got divorced, paid the wife off with about five million and bought himself a new black Porsche. My friend sent me round to his house and I got about three weeks' painting there.

On Monday evening I had fallen asleep on the sofa at home, and the client's mother, who had died four weeks before, woke me up and said "You are going to see my son. I need to speak to him, I really need to speak to him, it's very important and urgent."

I rang my friend up (he is a scientific type and doesn't believe in ghosts) and told him that I had the client's mum with me and she needed to speak to the client. He said "If you say one word you will never work for me again. People don't like to listen to your rubbish. Don't dare to say anything to this bloke because he's in a circle and they pass the names of good contractors on to one another." (Why did I ring him when I knew he doesn't believe? I suppose because I felt it would be dishonest not to.)

So ... I arrived at the client's house and his mum was with me and following me around. I was watching him uncertainly and the only conversation I had with him for three weeks was "Morning ………… See you tomorrow". All the while I was conscious of his mother's anxious presence and felt a real conflict of interest.

I had worked for three weeks and, towards the end of the third, he was packing to go away. On the last day, after I had finished painting, I was washing my rollers out in the bathroom. His mum was with me and I could also sense the guy was grieving, but privately. It looked as if we were going to be leaving at the same time.

Anyway, his mum pulled at my jumper and said "Come out of the bathroom; please let me speak to him, this is my last chance … please".

So I went up to him and said

"Look, I know this might sound weird but your mum's here and she needs to speak to you."

And he said "What? What are you on about?"

I said "Your mum's here right now".

He just stood there looking at me, and then he looked away. She was inside me now and she started talking non-stop to him for about two minutes.

Then he looked at me, called me "Mum" and started crying. Then his mum started crying, as did I and we were hugging each other.

I only remember bits of the conversation. The reason she had hung around was that he was going to do a deal with two friends and one of them was planning to take all the money that he had invested. Over the years his mother's advice had made him wealthy, she had been his mentor. Anyway she was saying goodbye to him for the last time and his mum and I hugged him and then she went.

He said "I'm going up north to do a deal right now with two friends. I got up this morning and walked through to the kitchen and thought 'Now what would mum do? Come on, do it, do the deal'. I can't believe this, I just spoke to my mum, I don't know how. I've got to tell my brothers I've just spoken to her. How long has she been with you?"

I said "Three weeks".

He said "I've been looking at you, thinking 'There's definitely something wrong with that bloke'. Why didn't you tell me?"

I said "Because my builder friend said that if I told you, I'd never get another job with him".

He hugged me again, shook my hand and said "Look, if my mum ever comes back, ring me up straight away."

I said "Your mother's gone, she won't come back."

At about eleven in the morning he drove off. He rang me the following day, in the evening at about ten o'clock at night. He said "I just wanted to say thanks - I didn't do the deal."

"That's ok."

In the meantime he had rung my friend up and said to him "Listen, if this guy hadn't said anything to me I'd have lost all my fortune."

In spite of the fact that the client was glad that I had told him about his mother - and the resultant saving of his fortune, my friend rang me up and said "I warned you, you won't be working for me again!" Maybe he felt he couldn't change his position, but I lost all the work I could have had with him.

*****

Two or more years later, my posh builder friend rang me up out of the blue and told me that he was stuck (couldn't find anyone free to give him a hand) and asked if I would help him in removing and replacing a spiral staircase in the basement of a big house in Kew. The staircase was massively heavy and was far too much for one person to deal with. As it happened, I was free so I said I would.

We met at the house, a huge old house filled with antiques of all kinds - furniture, big vases, that sort of thing. As we went into the house I felt something there and thought 'Oh no, please, not again!' We worked for some time taking the staircase apart and finally came to the bottom and the last few bolts. They wouldn't budge so my friend said that he had an angle grinder on another site and would fetch it - about twenty minutes. He left me on my own in the basement, to dismantle the last few bits which could be taken apart.

As soon as he had left the house, the basement door slammed shut and I could feel a presence getting closer and closer. I told it to get lost in no uncertain terms and, to my relief, it went. Seconds later I heard a loud smash on the ground floor and went up to discover that a large antique vase filled with lilies had fallen and smashed into hundreds of pieces, spilling water and lilies all over the floor. I thought 'Oh *no!*' - it was obviously a valuable object. As I was looking at the mess in dismay, my friend came back and asked what the hell I had been doing.

I told him what had happened but he didn't believe me, as his scientific outlook caused him to doubt such things. I asked him if he really thought that I would leave what I was doing in the basement and go upstairs, select an obviously valuable vase and smash it.

He said "No, I suppose not, but what am I going to tell the client?"

"The truth".

So he told the client what had happened. She believed him and said she would claim on her insurance ... but I never worked for him again.

*****

One evening, as we were going out for a meal, I suggested having a quick pint. My wife didn't want one but I insisted. We went into the pub and a woman, about fifty years old, was pouring me her first pint - she was new to the job and I was her first customer.

All of a sudden her husband got inside my body and said "Please, I need to speak to my wife right this second. Can you walk her through to the kitchen? Please, it's so urgent".

So I grabbed her hand and said "Could you stop that pint a minute? Can I have a quick word in the kitchen?" My wife just looked at us.

I took her into the kitchen, and her husband was in me, she could smell him - everything. I had all his pains, he had died of throat cancer but he must have had the disease elsewhere as well because I ached all over. I was puzzled by this because when you die you lose all your pain and you look the best you have ever looked. I have thought about it a lot since it happened and read about it too and I think that, when people grieve for too long, they hold their loved ones here, still with their pain, and they can't escape. I know it is difficult, but I think it is very important to have the courage and the kindness (and the love) to let them go, get rid of the pain and get on with what they need to do. There are spirits who hang around for their own reasons, as I have found out from one or two of the other encounters I have had. They know that they can be around and they can actually do things from the other side. Not a lot, but enough just to try to help the person they love, although those who stay of their own free will do not keep their pains. Only those who are kept here against their wishes do. Others are angry and want to inflict pain on those still living, like the spirit I talked about in Chapter

Three.

Anyway, he said to her (I can remember bits) "Please stop now, I want you to move on. Just go. Meet somebody else. I want you to. Stop this now, I want to go. This is my chance and you can let me go - right now".

His words and his voice were coming out of my mouth and she was saying goodbye to him and he was saying goodbye to her. Then he kissed her - and I found myself kissing this woman, this complete stranger.

Then the husband said "This is it, I'm going now. Just move on and meet somebody else, I want you to". He kissed her again and went. She just burst into tears.

She said "I can't believe this, I just spoke to him" and started crying.

Then I started crying and I thought

'Oh no, what do I tell my wife?'

I went out to the bar, walked round to where my wife was standing and the woman came running out, crying her eyes out, went round the bar and sat against the wall sobbing.

My wife said "What are you doing? What HAVE you been doing?"

I said "I don't know what I can tell you".

Once the woman had stopped crying, she came up and said "Thank you, that's what I needed".

(As I understand it, when you die it's up to you, it's your choice. If you want to go, you can go but if you don't want to go then you don't. So you've got the choice of going or staying. Most people (spirits) want to go in the end - enough's enough.)

The woman had been walking

around for seven years looking at the floor but after her husband talked to her through me she got on with her life. Now she has met somebody else and she rang me up and told me that she's doing really well. She sent me a text on New Year's Eve saying 'Always remember: Life is short. Break the rules. Forgive quickly. Kiss slowly. Love truly. Laugh uncontrollably. Never regret anything that made you smile.' She has sent me a text every New Year since.

*****

My brother asked me to paint his house in Feltham. One day when I was at the house, I went over the road to get some cigarettes and there was a woman sitting there dressed in sixties clothing. Really short skirt, big red lipstick, sitting cross-legged on the newspapers and I just looked over and I felt that she was more scared of me than I was of her. I had to look twice, but the second time I looked back I just knew that she was a spirit. I have no idea what she was doing or why she was just sitting there, but something told me not to interfere.

*****

While I was painting my brother's house a woman came up to me and said "Can you come and give me a price for decorating my house?"

I asked her where it was and she told me that it was just round the corner - a little bungalow.

I told her I couldn't come round that day but I would go round on my way to work the following morning.

At six o'clock the next morning I was still in bed and her husband appeared.

"What do you want?" I asked.

"You're coming to see my wife and I need to speak to her", was the reply.

I thought 'Oh no, not again'.

I told my wife that I had someone else with me again. She said "Well I don't want to know".

I drove over to Feltham and this guy was sitting in the passenger seat. It was really weird having him sitting there not saying a word - mind you I didn't want to talk to him anyway! He had died of cancer and his wife was having extreme difficulty in coming to terms with his death and could not let him go. So I got out of the car and her husband (I don't know how they do it and I don't want to know) just seemed to climb inside me. Each time it has happened the spirit seems to go round behind me and I feel a little jolt. It is a sort of warm feeling and, although my mind is still there and working, it seems as if I am sharing it and allowing the spirit to use it - and my mouth.

I knocked at the door and she said "Hello" and she came out.

I said "Look your husband's here and he needs to speak to you urgently".

"No!" She was very shocked.

I tried to reassure her: "He's here now, you hold my hand".

She said "Oh my God" and she could feel him, even smell him, and he began talking.

I was not aware of everything he said but I do remember him saying "Go and get my ashes and throw them away, just throw them. I don't want to be here, I want to go. You must let me go now so that you can get on with your life. I want to say goodbye to you now, please let me go".

"He wants to give you a kiss goodbye", I told her.

"What about the neighbours?" She asked.

"Forget the neighbours! Your husband's saying goodbye to you!"

So we kissed and hugged. We all three cried and he said goodbye.

Then she took me into the house … the whole house was a shrine to him. There were candles everywhere.

She showed me his urn and told me that she saw him every night, he would go upstairs before she went to bed. "Every night I've seen him and now he's gone".

While I was painting her house she kept asking me if I was sure he had gone and that she really wouldn't see him again.

I told her that he had really gone, that he had left after saying goodbye and that she should do as he asked and should take his ashes and scatter them somewhere. She said she would. You might expect that she would be sad that she wouldn't see him again but in fact it was a turning point for her.

*****

I had one experience with helping someone who was possessed by a malign spirit:

I was painting the house of a woman who, years earlier, had been involved in some kind of sect in the village she and her family had lived in. She had managed to escape with her children after the death of her husband but it had been an awful ordeal.

Anyway, one day she said "My daughter's quite disturbed, she's coming down tomorrow and you can see her. She's not well".

I asked what the problem was and she said "It's her head. She's had this headache for about eight years. She's a musician, a singer, living abroad".

The next day this really nice girl came into the room. She smiled at me but the smile didn't last very long. I just walked up to her and said "Come here". And I put my hand on her head and … it was bad. I got some really bad vibes. They were all down my body and it was fighting me - I was having a fight with whatever it was. And she said "Oogh! Phew!" Then she started smiling and her headache went. She had been possessed by a malign spirit that had invaded her body and was trying to take over her mind. I had to sit down for a while after that to make sure that my mind and body were clear of the spirit and when I got home I called on the light to help me be sure the unpleasant spirit was gone and that the experience had left me with no ill effects (see Chapter Ten). Every time I see her now she comes running up to me "Hello, hello" - I think she thinks I saved her life. Her possession had started in the village where everybody was involved in the above-mentioned sect.

Chapter Ten

The Light

I went to see the two women quite often after they helped me with the bitter spirit who tried to electrocute me (see Chapter Three) and they kept saying to me "Have you seen the light?" The light can be a source of energy (and spiritual cleansing) when it is needed.

"No".

"You will".

About three months later, my wife and I had gone out to a pub. I left her at the bar and was talking to some builders and I noticed she was talking to a man who was wearing gold everywhere: rings, chains, etc.

She asked him "Are you psychic?" She has no idea why she said that.

He said that he was and she said "So is my husband".

The bloke asked to meet me so she called me over and introduced me to him and the first words he said to me were "Have you seen the light?"

When I said I hadn't, he asked me if I wanted to and I said that I did.

He told me to go with him and we went to a corner and he put his hands on my shoulders and it seemed that he took me to Heaven and showed me the light. My whole body felt as if it were filled with light. It was an amazing feeling. He told me that now I should be able to find the light for myself whenever I felt the need.

I told the two ladies that I had seen the light and they were pleased and reminded me that they had told me I would. I am still friends with the man who showed me the light, who is also a healer. He says that if he had my power he would be rich - a millionaire! But that is not the way it works ... for me anyway. Several people have suggested I could make a lot of money if I asked for it; but if I did that I wouldn't have a goal in my life any more and to have a goal is very important. I also have this feeling that if I asked for money then my power would withdraw and I don't want that to happen. Some people have even suggested I should ask the spirits for the lottery numbers but I'm sure they wouldn't give them to me!

Since that day I can, at any time during the day, sit or lie down and go to what seems like Heaven to me. I watch through all the colour changes - the blues, the greens and the oranges. They are like bubbles that burst. The colours just blow you away and my eyes follow them round. One disappears and another bubble of colour comes and gradually you go through all the colours of the rainbow and when you get to the yellows, they get lighter and lighter and slowly they get so light that they turn to white. And then, when it's all white, (most of the time I am lying on my bed when I do this) there is a person, an angel, floating above me who takes my hands and sends this massive energy through my hands and into my body.

The first time it happened, I got up after a second because I didn't like it, I got really scared, and I went back downstairs. The following day I went back upstairs again and tried it again and I lasted ten seconds with this energy and I still got a bit scared. The third time I tried it I psyched myself right up for it and I went up to my bedroom and lay there and thought 'Now I'm going to take this'. I lay there and went through all the stages of the colours and got to the yellows and I felt that I was in Heaven and the charge came and this one really shook me but I was ready and waiting for it. I just went rigid, I couldn't move, but I let it happen. And the energy, which was so beautiful, went through my hands and I loved it. I thought I was going to cry. It lasted about five minutes. It just stops - it knows when I have had enough. Then everything becomes normal again.

Sometimes when I have a Saturday off and I'm tired after a hectic week, I get up, go out and get some rolls for the kids, get the papers, do a few things and about eleven or twelve o'clock I might go up and have an hour's nap if I need it. Occasionally, when I am having my nap, the colour bubbles appear and I can now tell them in my head that I want to go to sleep and they just shut off. Sometimes they come back.

Now all the spirits who are still stuck here see my light and they think it's their guiding light but it is not. My light is for healing.

Chapter Eleven

Learning to Shut Down

Most of the encounters I have had with spirits, other than those where the spirit wanted my help, have not had any physical effects even though they have not been particularly pleasant experiences - although one or two have been quite amusing:

I know several people with gifts like mine - four locally, the two ladies, the guy who showed me the light and my psychic school friend, Scatty. I grew up with her at school, but we never really spoke until a couple of years ago when there was a man, a spirit, standing behind me at the bar in the pub. (I can handle that, I just get into conversation with people around me - although my hair stands on end!)

Scatty said "Do you mind if I join in the conversation?"

When I asked what she meant she said "The man behind you".

I said "Oh, can you see him?"

"Yes, tell him to go away".

"I can't do that"

She said "I can" ... and she did ... and he went away.

For a long time if I went in there for more than half an hour he would visit me about three or four times - standing behind me or next to me. I have absolutely no idea why he should have chosen to join me at the bar! My friends knew when he was there because all my hair would stand on end.

Now I've learnt to say in my head

"Go away" and he does. Sometimes I can just cough and he'll go away which is quite funny really.

*****

I was painting some offices in London for a very nice chap who told me that he was so impressed with my work he would like me to paint his bungalow for him. He asked me if I travelled any distance to work and I said I did not. He said that it wasn't far, only to Guildford, but I still said no.

I was working at his offices for some time and he persisted, politely and I kept saying that I wouldn't until finally I thought 'Oh well, why not?' I was booked solid for six months so I asked him if he could wait for six months and he said he could! He told me that since he and his wife had moved into the bungalow they had been having a lot of work done and had had endless trouble and problems with workmen: plumbers, electricians, carpenters, painters, and they had not been able to get any of the work finished. I thought that it sounded rather odd but decided that I would give it a go.

After the six months I phoned him and arranged to start work. When I got there I thought 'Oh no, there is something nasty in this house'. Anyway, I met the wife and was talking to them both; they were very nice, courteous people. They told me a little more about the problems they had had and about the previous painter. He had been painting a door and had turned round to the wife and, as he did so, his head had turned into the head of a fox and he had bared his teeth and snarled a chuckle at her. I should have realised that something was seriously amiss when they told me about that - it obviously wasn't the workman but some nasty spirit in the house. He did no more painting there and the job remained unfinished which was why I had been asked to do the work. They showed me round - all the bits that were unfinished.

At the end of the day, I told them that I was sure that there was a malign spirit in their bungalow and asked if they would like me to get in touch with a couple I knew of who specialise in getting rid of such unwelcome presences. They agreed and this couple drove all the way from Devon. They are elderly and make no charge. They spent quite a while and then said that once I had finished painting the front room, which I was working on at the time (two shades of grey!), the spirit would leave.

I worked at the bungalow for a week and had almost finished painting the front room, I would finish it on the Monday. Things were beginning to go wrong … my family were squabbling and when I came to start the car on the Monday it wouldn't work no matter what I did. My only choice was to take the train. I did this and phoned the client's wife from Guildford station and explained what had happened. She agreed to come and fetch me. When she arrived I got in the car and we set off.

After a few minutes she turned to me and snarled in a gravelly male voice "Why didn't you phone me from home?" I didn't know what to say. We continued the short journey in silence. I was very taken aback as this was not like her at all.

Anyway, I started arranging my dust sheets ready to start the final bit of painting in the front room and she came into the room, walked right up close to me, stuck her face almost against mine and snarled in the same gravelly, man's voice "Get the hell out of my house right now. Get your things and get out". I started to say something as I realised that this was the malign spirit speaking - no way was he going to let me finish painting the room as he would have to leave. She wouldn't let me speak.

I had a real problem because here I was with no car and all my gear there - dust sheets, paint trays, brushes, masking tape, white spirit and all the rest. Anyway, I left and managed to make my way home. When I got there I found chaos - a fight between one of my boys and my daughter and a general air of discomfort and unease … not my home at all!

This was back to aggression like the attempt to electrocute me but worse because it was transferring to my family.

I phoned my friend Scatty and said I really needed her help and explained the problem. The first thing she said was "Have you got the guy's telephone number on your mobile? If so, delete it". She said that the entity had followed me home via my mobile! I deleted the number immediately. She told me she couldn't come round that day but would be there tomorrow and that I should make sure that everyone else was out of the house.

The next day I had great difficulty in getting everyone out of the house, everybody seemed to be in a foul, unco-operative mood. I managed it and then Scatty arrived. She found where the thing was and told me to go outside, which I did but left the door slightly open just in case. I heard her tell it to go and it replied, in the same gravelly man's voice I had heard in Guildford, that it wouldn't. Scatty was very firm but he resisted, even started bringing the walls together to squash her. He was very strong but so is she and, after a while I felt a wind brush past me and the door slammed shut with terrific force.

The following day I thought I should phone the husband and tell him what had happened and offer to get the couple from Devon to come back.

I phoned him and said "Good morning, this is ..." the familiar gravelly man's voice interrupted me, snarling "I know who you are". So I put the phone down and that was that. I feel very sorry for them and often wonder whether they are still in the bungalow, but I had to consider my family and, thanks to Scatty, the spirit was out of my life. I had to accept that I had done the best I could do.

*****

That spirit had affected the owners of a house spiritually. I think that sometimes a spirit can affect the people in a house physically as well:

I was painting a house which had a spirit in the bathroom - a teenage boy had hanged himself there and made his presence felt to me … I couldn't use the bathroom and had to go to a nearby pub to answer 'calls of nature'. I was dreading having to paint that room, the boy didn't want to talk to me so I couldn't send him on his way as I have done with some others.

The owners worked from home and the man was a very jealous person. I had noticed that the woman kept rubbing her neck and could hardly move it. One day when her husband had gone out to get some more paint, I asked her if she would like me to heal it for her. She said it would have to be quick and we would have to stand by the window so she could see when her husband returned. I put my hand on her neck for about four minutes and she smiled and started to move her head quite freely.

The job took about a week and at last I had to paint the bathroom. Normally it would have taken a full day to do, but I worked at lightning speed and got it done in three hours - a most uncomfortable three hours. I'm not sure why there was no interference from the boy, but it could be that I was subconsciously learning to shut down. I was, at last, going to achieve it after this next, multi-spirit, experience!

*****

A few years ago a builder friend of mine asked me if I was up for working at Hampton Court (he knows that I have sometimes had troubles with encountering spirits in places where I have worked). When I said that I thought it should be all right, he asked if I wanted a trial run because the place is really, really haunted. He said "We'll take you to have a quick look and then you can start the following day". So we got there about

6.30 - 6.45 and we were working on one of the first bits ever built by Henry VIII - the Real Tennis courts, which are still there now. People still play on them but they are all royal guests. We were working on the apartments which were built in 1503. Can you imagine painting a building that old?

The builder said to me "I'll go and get the alarm switched off and you go and get the coffees. You go in through that entrance and you'll find a machine". I said "OK".

It was dark and it was black. He was going to be away about five or ten minutes - I knew that because it was quite some distance. So I walked into the entrance which is called Tennis Court Alley - a massive entrance as big as a room. I just casually walked in - I didn't even think of anything. As I walked in I saw that there were about fifteen people in costumes, all talking. But the idea of fifteen spirits (usually you just get one and that's plenty!) threw me back and I thought '*#+<>!' ... and they seemed to have exactly the same reaction to me - they fell silent and just looked at me.

I legged it, there were too many for me. One's all right, but not fifteen of them - all in 15th or 16th century costume. The fact that I ran from them made this the second worst experience I've had with ghosts; I didn't feel good about that. Thinking about it afterwards, I felt that I should have stood my ground and looked back at them ... maybe I could have helped them 'move on'.

After that I thought that I couldn't cope with so many spirits all at once and I really had to learn to shut down. Scatty had been telling me "You know you must shut down, you're open all the time, that's why they keep coming at you."

Even the guy who showed me the light told me that I must shut down. He told me that before he learnt how to do it, he used to have a ghost in his home who would walk through the wall, sit down on the sofa beside him, watch telly with him for about half an hour and then go back through the wall. The ghost wouldn't talk even when the guy asked him what he wanted. There was also a boy in his bathroom and when he asked him why he didn't walk round the house a bit instead of just staying in the bathroom he wouldn't move. This is what happens with some spirits, they just want to stay in the same place. Some want to be rescued (helped to go on their way to the light and what lies ahead) and some don't.

I told the builder that the coffee machine wasn't working - I didn't want to tell him I'd run from the 'ghosts'. I did the job. You can learn to shut down and at Hampton Court I learned how to do it, how to switch off. Somehow in your mind you construct an invisible shield round you which is impenetrable. I used to walk round the building in my lunch break, practising. I knew they were there - everywhere. I'd say in that building there must be upwards of a hundred ghosts from the sixteenth and seventeenth centuries - they are wearing Elizabethan clothes. I don't think I'd like to be there on my own in the evening! They all seem to be standing around talking in the corridors, which appears to be where they meet. But that's down here and these are spirits who either don't know they have died or prefer to stay here.

*****

Many people have had experiences of almost dying, some have told of what happened before they were 'sent back'. I think that in Heaven, we meet up with all our friends and loved ones. When we die there's someone we love waiting for us as we get there and everywhere is filled with light. We're taken to a house which appears exactly the same as our own house and there are the people who have passed away - all our friends and relations. We are going to somewhere where we are really welcome and we stay there until we have recovered from the shock of dying and are ready to move on. There are things that, as spirits, we want to do and learn so that we can develop. I know that must seem weird, but it's a continuation of life, but without our bodies. So people who are frightened of dying needn't be.

PART TWO

A number of my 'patients' have themselves written about what happened and some of their stories are included in the main section of this book to enlarge upon my own account. Some experiences of healing people I haven't talked about because there have been so many (probably several hundred I think) and I don't remember all of them - only those which, for some reason have stood out in my memory. A few of those I haven't mentioned have written their own accounts of what happened and these I have put into this section.

Chapter Twelve

"Patients" at Work

As you may imagine, working with builders and given the nature of the job they do, many of my work acquaintances have a wide variety of pains and injuries. So ... when I am employed on that sort of job I often have to give healing to several of my workmates. Here is a selection of such episodes which some of them have written about:

Denis Turner, a plumber, says:

"I suffered with a shoulder problem for approximately two years. The doctor suggested that rest was the best cure. Being a builder with a family to support, this was not possible. I could not afford to have time off work.

The pain got worse. It kept me awake at night.

I bumped into Pinky in a café one day and told him my problem. I had heard of his healing powers, but I never believed in any of it. Anyway, he put his hand on my shoulder for about five minutes. I felt a warm tingling sensation in my shoulder. The pain had gone. I could not believe it.

I arranged to see him again in a week's time. The same thing happened. That was in October 2007 and to this day I am completely free of pain and can work normally again.

Cheers Pinky."

Trevor Clark is a window cleaner and tells his story:

"I was working on a job in East Sheen. It had been raining and my ladders were wet. When I went to raise my ladder to the first floor window it didn't secure properly and as I let it go, it slipped six feet and hit the palm of my left hand leaving a one and a half inch gash. This caused my ring finger to get stuck in a spasm. I managed to finish the job, but my ring finger didn't straighten and I was concerned about it so I booked an appointment to see my doctor.

The doctor confirmed my fears and told me that I had damaged my tendon and that only time would correct it.

A week later the wound had healed but that left a raised mound of scar tissue and my finger still stuck in spasm. To cut a long story short, I met Pinky on a night out in a local pub and he said that he could heal me. He told me to bring a lemonade and an orange juice, so I did. He then rested his hand on the palm of my hand and it started to get warm. Then slowly my finger started to straighten and after a while the lump of scar tissue in the palm of my hand started to go down as if by magic."

Steve, a painter, says:

"Well, Pink, I would like to start by saying thank you for being a good man - that is how you helped me. On the first day I worked with you I was much more relaxed than I would have been on my own. You put your hand on my side where I had a dull pain which had been there for about two and a half years. The pain eased and I don't have that problem any more which made me feel more at ease with myself.

You not only helped the pain in my stomach but in my head too - you have a positive and calming way that has helped me get through this tough time. You see the right in people and know the wrong. You look at things from many angles all at the same time and know how to come out with the right answer very quickly - and that is an art in itself. I know how real you are because I can see in your face that you really have taken pain away from people and that you are a genuine man.

I have been a very lucky man to have had a sort of counsellor working with me. Every building site should have one - in fact you should be everywhere! You are considerate and that's what this world needs more of and you have inspired me to be nice and what more could anyone want? You will always be my friend."

This is the story of Jonathan Price, an electrician:

"I'm a pretty fit young bloke, so I have not had many problems regarding my health. I'm an electrician so I use my hands a lot of the time. Over the years I have developed a really sharp pain in my left wrist. I first met Pink through a friend.

We were having breakfast and I had mentioned my wrist pain. Pink didn't say much. Then, after ten minutes, he asked me to give him my wrist. His hand was very warm. He placed his hand over my wrist and left it there for one or two minutes and the pain was gone.

That was two years ago. Just recently my wrist was starting to hurt again. I have just started work on a massive job in Surbiton and Pink is on the same job. I told him about my wrist and he gave me a five minute session. The next day the pain had gone. It's totally strange and I can't explain it but, hand on my heart, he has got rid of all pain in my wrist. I'll always keep his number on my phone and I'll be ringing him before I go skiing next year."

Chapter Thirteen

Accounts Written by 'Patients'

Jackie Worth contributes:

"Pinky's Hands"

"I believe it was in the winter of 2006/2007. My husband and I were visiting with friends at a pub in Richmond. It was near the end of a six or eight week stay in London and I had been having trouble with my back after a lot of walking and not always sleeping on the best of mattresses. After alternately standing and sitting at the bar whilst chatting with friends, I kept shifting about, trying to find a comfortable position to relieve the pain in my back.

Pinky must have noticed something because he came over and introduced himself, asking if I was having back trouble. Actually, it was more a case of him telling me that I was in pain. I confirmed his analysis. He then explained that he had some skills as a healer and offered to help me, "lay on hands" as it were. Well, I was sceptical. But what was there to lose?

He pressed his hand on my lower back and almost immediately I felt an intense warming in that area. It must be admitted that for the rest of the afternoon the pain was gone, so initially I was impressed. I was astounded, a day or two later when flying back to the States, to find I had absolutely no back trouble at all even whilst sitting in economy. For another week after that I had no trouble. Sadly, as can happen with other forms of alternative medicine like hypnosis and acupuncture, the healing effects faded after that. I look forward to meeting Pinky at the pub next time I am in Richmond to thank him for that pain-free week and perhaps to get a follow-up healing session".

Kathy Morrison writes:

"For the past couple of years I have had problems on and off with neck pain which quite often travels down one or both arms.

On the day I received healing my neck had been particularly achy and uncomfortable for about three weeks and I had referred pain travelling down both arms.

Pinky simply held his hand on the back of my neck and I wasn't aware of any sensations from the healing at the time. By the evening I was aware that my neck felt completely pain free and by the following day I had no arm pain either.

Since then I have had no further

pain in either of these areas.

How wonderful.

Josie tells us:

"I have known Pinky for many years. One day I just happened to meet him at our local supermarket. We stopped and chatted for a while about things in general, not about anything to do with health problems. Then, just as I was leaving, he said to me

"Promise me something. When you go home, look in the mirror and say 'I love you' and do this every day."

I didn't know why he had said this, but I did it anyway and every time I saw Pinky, even if he was across the road, he would say "I love you".

It was after quite a while that I realised why he had said that to me. I had had problems with my eyes due to having a thyroid disorder.

Soon after meeting Pinky in the supermarket my eyes were not swollen or watering any more and looked normal. Pinky had not mentioned my eyes but I think he knew just how much it got me down, so thanks Pinky, for caring."

Paula More writes:

I had always painted my various homes myself as I enjoyed creating a transformation but though my current one desperately needed attention, I was frustrated by a 'frozen shoulder'. I had been having treatment for it for months but, though a little better, I could not move my arm freely or without pain. A friend suggested that I should ask Pinky for a quote to do the work. He came round to assess the job and while he was doing so, I told him that I usually did it myself but had a bad shoulder. He gave me a quote, which I accepted, and we arranged that he should start the following week. As I was about to open the front door for him he said "Stand still" and put his hand on my shoulder for about three minutes. His hand grew very hot and I felt a warm tingling in my shoulder. When he took his hand away I said "Thank you" and he told me to say 'thank you' to whatever/whoever I believed in before going to sleep, he said that that would allow the healing to continue.

For several hours afterwards I could still feel his hand on my shoulder, which improved during the rest of the day and the following morning was very much better.

During the week he was painting my home (which now looks great - he is a very fine craftsman and does a beautiful job) he gave me some more healing sessions - on my neck and shoulder. He also gave me healing for my elbow, which I damaged years ago and ever since had had extreme difficulty in writing. Since then I have had no further problem and, for the first time in about fifteen years, can write with ease. 'Wonderful' is a gross understatement ... but there's more:

Many years ago I, too, was a healer but, due to pressure of work and a number of other causes and preoccupations, had not healed anyone for a long time and so had, I thought, lost the gift. During that week, whilst having coffee and lunch, Pinky and I talked a lot and, to my great surprise and delight, I gradually became aware that the power was reawakening and so it has proved. My (re)developing gift is nowhere near as strong as his but it is wonderful to be able to help people again.

Pinky is a gentle, warm and very unassuming man yet he has a strangely compelling "presence" which should tell those with eyes to see that he is gifted and that there is much more to him than appears at first sight.

I am hugely indebted to Pinky and will always be grateful to him for what he has done for me and for his friendship.

And finally:

Patrick Masterson recalls:

"The first time I heard of Pinky was about eight months before I met him - four years ago. Several mutual friends and acquaintances, as well as others whom I did not know so well, talked of this man who had the power of healing. Being a natural sceptic I decided to take what I had heard with a pinch of salt! Nevertheless, these rumours and professions of faith in his ability to heal persisted. One day I was talking to a very good friend of mine who was convinced that Pinky had the power to heal. He had seen this at work and remarked at some length on the client's reaction. The results were immediate and the client was visibly amazed. No more acute pains - nor coughing up of blood. Naturally I was now intrigued.

About a fortnight after this conversation, I was introduced to Pinky through this friend of mine. I expected to see a commanding, charismatic man who would engage people by his immediate presence. Instead he appeared to be a quite ordinary, humble and self-effacing person. However, I was aware that his handshake was warm and I was taken by his kindly demeanour. After a few moments, he told me I was 'quite ill'. He told me then that his handshake was enough to inform him of this.

He persisted in asking me questions concerning my health. I answered as honestly as I could. Abruptly he placed the palm and outstretched fingers of his right hand over and just below the right side of my ribs for about thirty or forty seconds. I experienced a warm sensation and a tremendous feeling of ease with a sense of well-being. Pinky then told me to say 'thank you' in my own particular way just before I went to sleep. He said that, if I had my own God or a spiritual understanding of the meaning of this, then I should use this as a focus when saying 'thank you'. He was adamant that it was not him I had to thank.

I thought it significant that he

called his rare gift an affliction that he has to bear. This conveyed to me the stamp of the man as being 'down to earth' with a 'no-nonsense' attitude to life. He said he could not understand why he was either chosen or was blessed with this ability. At no point throughout our conversation did he say that it was he who had made it possible for people to be healed.

On a more personal note, for about eighteen months I was on a liver transplant list and did not show signs of recovery nor stability within this condition. On one occasion I was brought into hospital as a liver (for my size) was available. However, another patient whose need was greater than mine received this liver.

Shortly after this, I met Pinky in Sainsbury's. He shook me warmly by the hand and we exchanged our news. Not long afterwards my health had reached its nadir. My brother had died tragically over this period and depression had set in quite deeply. I bumped into Pinky and he told me that he was quite concerned for me. He rested his palm over the same area as before. We then shook hands and he wished me luck.

By degrees, though not immediately, my health improved. After six months my health and liver function started to improve dramatically; so much so that I was taken off the transplant list six months later. I am not saying that this positive change in my health was down to Pinky; however, the coincidence of meeting him and consequent improvement is uncanny to say the least.

Pinky and I do not often mix socially though we both get on splendidly. I know he likes me and, I guess, he likes most people. In fact I can honestly say that I have yet to meet anyone who speaks of him in derogatory terms. Plainly, he sees good in people, recognises their frailties and flaws and speaks in positive terms about them.

He has certainly given me a renewed faith in myself and the importance of being in touch with my inner self. He gave me hope throughout my recovery. Finally, his love and warmth washed over me and, in a lot of ways, made me a better, more caring person.

ACKNOWLEDGEMENTS

I would like to thank a number of special people who have helped me through both the good and the hard times: my parents, whose love set me on the right path; my beautiful wife and my family who have stood by me even when I seemed to be 'losing the plot' - having psychological struggles; my brother; C.B. and Scatty.

I am very grateful to those kind people who have contributed their own accounts of what happened when I gave them healing.

My grateful thanks go to those who have helped with the writing of this book: Jonathan Price; Bee and Hugo without whose encouragement the book would not have been written. Several people have read the book and made excellent suggestions for improvement. Some have given considerable time and thought to writing annotations and suggestions. They know who they are and to all of them Pippin and I are most deeply grateful.

Finally and above all, my thanks to Pippin … who wrote it.